THE ULTIMATED

AFFILIATE

MARKETING GUIDE

By

JOEL K. JOHN

Table Of Content

Introduction to Affiliate Marketing

Affiliate marketing is a popular and lucrative online business model that allows individuals to earn passive income by promoting products or services offered by other companies. It is a performance-based marketing strategy where affiliates (also known as publishers) earn a commission for each sale or lead generated through their marketing efforts.

In the affiliate marketing ecosystem, there are three key players: the merchant (also known as the advertiser or vendor), the affiliate, and the customer. The merchant is the company or individual that creates or provides the product or service. The affiliate acts as a middleman, promoting the merchant's offerings through various marketing channels. The customer is the end-user who makes a purchase or takes a desired action.

The concept of affiliate marketing revolves around the use of affiliate links. These unique tracking links contain an affiliate's unique identifier, allowing the merchant to track and attribute sales or conversions generated by the affiliate's promotional efforts. When a customer clicks on an affiliate link and completes a desired action, such as making a purchase or filling out a form, the affiliate earns a commission.

One of the key advantages of affiliate marketing is its low barrier to entry. Anyone can become an affiliate marketer, regardless of their background or experience. It offers a flexible and scalable business opportunity that can be pursued full-time or as a side income stream.

Affiliates have the freedom to choose the products or services they want to promote, allowing them to align their efforts with their interests and expertise.

Affiliate marketing operates on a performance-based model, making it a win-win situation for both affiliates and merchants. Affiliates have the potential to earn a significant income based on their marketing efforts, while merchants benefit from increased brand exposure, lead generation, and sales without incurring upfront marketing costs.

To succeed in affiliate marketing, it is essential to understand the target audience, select profitable niches, and choose reputable affiliate programs. Additionally, effective marketing strategies, such as content creation, search engine optimization (SEO), social media marketing, and email marketing, play a crucial role in driving traffic and conversions.

As with any business endeavor, affiliate marketing requires dedication, perseverance, and continuous learning. By leveraging the right strategies, building strong relationships with the audience, and staying up-to-date with industry trends, aspiring affiliate marketers can establish a profitable online business and achieve long-term success.

Remember, affiliate marketing is not a get-rich-quick scheme. It requires effort, strategic planning, and a commitment to providing value to your audience. With the right mindset and a willingness to learn and adapt, you can embark on an exciting journey as an affiliate marketer and unlock the potential for financial freedom and flexibility.

Key Concepts and Terminology in Affiliate Marketing

To navigate the world of affiliate marketing effectively, it's important to familiarize yourself with key concepts and terminology that are commonly used in the industry. Understanding these terms will not only help you communicate with other affiliates and merchants but also enable you to make informed decisions and optimize your affiliate marketing efforts. *Here are some essential concepts and terms to know*:

Affiliate: An individual or entity that promotes products or services offered by merchants in exchange for a commission.

Merchant/Advertiser/Vendor: The company or individual that creates or provides the product or service that affiliates promote.

Affiliate Network: An intermediary platform that connects affiliates with merchants, providing a centralized system for tracking, reporting, and managing affiliate programs.

Affiliate Program: A structured arrangement offered by merchants that outlines the terms and conditions for affiliates, including commission rates, payment schedules, and marketing guidelines.

Affiliate Link: A unique URL provided to affiliates that contains their unique identifier, allowing the merchant to track sales or conversions generated by the affiliate's marketing efforts.

Commission: The percentage or fixed amount of money an affiliate earns for each sale or action generated through their affiliate link.

Conversion: The desired action taken by a customer, such as making a purchase, signing up for a newsletter, or filling out a form, resulting in a commission for the affiliate.

Click-Through Rate (CTR): The percentage of people who click on an affiliate link compared to the total number of people who view the link.

Cost Per Action (CPA): An affiliate marketing model where affiliates earn a commission when a specific action, such as a sale or lead, is generated.

Cost Per Click (CPC): An affiliate marketing model where affiliates earn a commission based on the number of clicks their affiliate links receive, regardless of whether a conversion occurs.

Earnings Per Click (EPC): The average amount of money an affiliate earns per click on their affiliate links, calculated by dividing total earnings by the number of clicks.

Landing Page: The web page where a visitor is directed after clicking on an affiliate link, designed to encourage conversions and provide relevant information about the promoted product or service.

Cookies: Small text files stored on a user's device when they visit a website, used to track affiliate referrals and attribute sales or conversions to the respective affiliates.

Affiliate Manager: A representative from the merchant or affiliate network who assists affiliates with program-related inquiries, provides support, and helps optimize their marketing efforts.

Sub-Affiliate: An affiliate recruited by another affiliate, earning a portion of the commission generated by the sub-affiliate's promotional activities.

By understanding these key concepts and familiarizing yourself with the associated terminology, you'll be better equipped to navigate the affiliate marketing landscape, engage in meaningful discussions, and optimize your strategies for success.

Overview of the Affiliate Marketing Ecosystem

The affiliate marketing ecosystem is a dynamic and interconnected network that involves various stakeholders, processes, and technologies. Understanding the different elements within this ecosystem is crucial for affiliate marketers to effectively navigate and succeed in the industry. ***Here's an overview of the key components***:

Merchants/Advertisers: Merchants, also known as advertisers or vendors, are businesses or individuals who create or provide products or services. They utilize affiliate marketing as a cost-effective way to expand their reach, increase brand exposure, and drive sales or desired actions.

Affiliates/Publishers: Affiliates, also known as publishers, are individuals or entities who promote the products or services of merchants through various marketing channels. Affiliates earn a commission for each successful sale or conversion generated through their marketing efforts.

Affiliate Networks: Affiliate networks act as intermediaries between affiliates and merchants. They provide a platform where merchants can list their affiliate programs, and affiliates can discover and join programs. Affiliate networks also facilitate tracking, reporting, and payment processes.

Affiliate Programs: Affiliate programs are structured arrangements offered by merchants to attract and incentivize affiliates to promote their products or services. These programs outline the commission structure, promotional guidelines, tracking mechanisms, and other terms and conditions for affiliates.

Affiliate Links: Affiliates receive unique tracking links, also known as affiliate links, from merchants or affiliate networks. These links contain the affiliate's unique identifier, allowing the merchant to track and attribute sales or conversions generated by the affiliate's promotional efforts.

Customers: Customers are the end-users who engage with the affiliate's promotional content and make a purchase or take a desired action. They may click on an affiliate link, visit the merchant's website, and complete a transaction, resulting in a commission for the affiliate.

Tracking and Attribution: Tracking technologies, such as cookies or other tracking mechanisms, are used to attribute sales or conversions to the respective affiliates. This ensures that affiliates receive proper credit for the traffic they drive and the actions they generate.

Commission Structures: Merchants define commission structures, specifying the percentage or fixed amount of money that affiliates earn for each successful sale or conversion. Commission rates can vary based on the type of product or service, the affiliate's performance, or other factors.

Reporting and Analytics: Affiliate networks or tracking tools provide reporting and analytics features, enabling affiliates to monitor their performance, track earnings, and optimize their marketing strategies based on data insights.

Payments: Affiliate networks or merchants handle the payment process, disbursing commissions to affiliates based on the agreed-upon payment schedule and thresholds. Payment methods can vary, including bank transfers, PayPal, or other digital payment platforms.

Compliance and Regulations: Affiliate marketing is subject to various compliance regulations, such as disclosing affiliate relationships and adhering to guidelines set by regulatory bodies like the Federal Trade Commission (FTC). Affiliates must ensure they comply with these regulations to maintain transparency and ethical practices.

Tools and Technologies: Various tools and technologies, such as content management systems, SEO plugins, social media schedulers, and tracking software, assist affiliates in managing and optimizing their affiliate marketing activities.

Understanding the interplay between these elements is essential for affiliate marketers to build successful partnerships, effectively promote products or services, and generate revenue. By leveraging the affiliate marketing ecosystem and implementing effective strategies, affiliates can create a sustainable and profitable business model.

Chapter 2: Finding Your Niche

Identifying Your Interests and Passions

When embarking on the journey of affiliate marketing, one of the crucial steps in finding success is identifying your interests and passions. Your personal interests can serve as a solid foundation for building a sustainable and fulfilling affiliate marketing business. *Here's why identifying your interests and passions matters*:

Motivation and Enjoyment: Affiliate marketing requires dedication, time, and effort. When you choose a niche aligned with your interests and passions, you'll find yourself motivated and enthusiastic about the content you create and the products you promote. This motivation will help you stay committed and consistently produce valuable content for your audience.

Authenticity and Credibility: Being genuinely passionate about your niche allows you to showcase your authentic voice and expertise. Your passion will shine through in your content and promotions, establishing trust with your audience. People are more likely to trust recommendations from someone who is passionate and knowledgeable about a topic.

Content Creation: As an affiliate marketer, creating high-quality content is vital. When you are passionate about your niche, generating content becomes more enjoyable and easier. You'll have a wealth of ideas and insights to share, making your content engaging, informative, and valuable to your audience.

Targeting the Right Audience: Your interests and passions can guide you in identifying and understanding your target audience. Since you have a genuine interest in the niche, you are more likely to understand the needs, challenges, and preferences of your audience. This understanding will enable you to tailor your content and promotions to effectively resonate with your target market.

Long-Term Sustainability: Affiliate marketing is a long-term endeavor. By selecting a niche that genuinely interests you, you are more likely to sustain your business in the long run. Your passion will help you overcome challenges, adapt to industry changes, and continually provide value to your audience.

***To identify your interests and passions, consider the following steps**:*

Self-Reflection: Take some time to reflect on your hobbies, personal interests, and areas of expertise. What topics do you enjoy learning about or discussing with others? What activities bring you joy and fulfillment? Identifying these areas will help you narrow down potential niches.

Market Research: Conduct market research to validate the profitability and demand for potential niches aligned with your interests. Look for niches that have a target audience with purchasing power and a need for products or services. Explore online communities, forums, and social media platforms to gauge the level of interest and engagement in those niches.

Competition Analysis: Analyze the competition within your potential niches. Look for gaps or opportunities where you can provide a unique perspective or differentiate yourself from existing affiliates. Find a balance between niches with ample demand and competition that allows you to stand out.

Alignment with Affiliate Programs: Research affiliate programs related to your chosen niches. Ensure that there are suitable affiliate programs that align with your interests and offer products or services you believe in. Look for reputable merchants with attractive commission structures and affiliate-friendly policies.

Remember that identifying your interests and passions is just the first step. It's equally important to conduct thorough market research, understand your target audience, and develop effective marketing strategies to succeed as an affiliate marketer.

By aligning your business with your passions, you'll not only enjoy the process but also have a higher chance of building a successful and fulfilling affiliate marketing venture.

Conducting Market Research

Market research is a critical step in affiliate marketing that allows you to gather valuable insights about your target audience, competition, and industry trends. By conducting thorough market research, you can make informed decisions, refine your affiliate marketing strategies, and maximize your chances of success. ***Here's a guide on how to conduct effective market research:***

Define Your Target Audience: Start by clearly defining your target audience. Understand their demographics, interests, needs, and preferences. Determine the specific problems or challenges they face that your affiliate marketing efforts can help solve. This knowledge will guide your content creation and promotional strategies.

Explore Online Communities and Forums: Participate in online communities, forums, and social media groups related to your niche. Observe discussions, questions, and comments from your target audience. This will provide valuable insights into their pain points, interests, and the type of content they seek. Take note of popular topics and recurring questions that can guide your content creation.

Use Keyword Research Tools: Keyword research tools like Google Keyword Planner, SEMrush, or Ahrefs can help you understand the search volume and competitiveness of keywords related to your niche. Identify high-volume keywords that align with your content strategy, as these can drive organic traffic to your affiliate site.

Analyze Competitors: Analyzing your competitors is crucial to identify their strengths, weaknesses, and gaps in the market that you can capitalize on. Visit competitor websites, blogs, and social media profiles. Study their content, promotions, audience engagement, and the products or services they promote. Identify areas where you can provide a unique value proposition or differentiate yourself from competitors.

Research Affiliate Programs: Explore affiliate programs within your niche. Look for reputable affiliate networks or individual merchants that offer products or services aligned with your audience's needs. Assess commission structures, payment terms, affiliate support, and the overall reputation of the affiliate programs. Choose programs that provide fair compensation and a positive affiliate experience.

Stay Updated with Industry Trends: Stay informed about industry trends, innovations, and emerging technologies within your niche. Follow industry blogs, news websites, podcasts, and thought leaders in your field. Understanding the current and future trends will help you adapt your strategies, capitalize on new opportunities, and stay ahead of the competition.

Analyze Data and Track Performance: Utilize analytics tools, such as Google Analytics, to track and analyze data related to your website's traffic, user behavior, and conversions. This data will provide insights into the effectiveness of your marketing campaigns, popular content, and areas for improvement.

Regularly monitor and analyze data to optimize your affiliate marketing efforts.

Remember, market research is an ongoing process. As your affiliate marketing business evolves, continue to gather feedback from your audience, adapt to changes in the market, and refine your strategies accordingly. By conducting thorough market research, you'll be equipped with the knowledge and insights to effectively target your audience, create compelling content, and promote the right products or services, ultimately maximizing your success as an affiliate marketer.

Selecting a Profitable Niche for Affiliate Marketing

Choosing a profitable niche is a crucial step in building a successful affiliate marketing business. A niche refers to a specific segment or area of interest within a broader market. By selecting a profitable niche, you can target a specific audience, create focused content, and increase your chances of generating substantial income. *Here are some key factors to consider when selecting a profitable niche for affiliate marketing*:

Passion and Interest: Start by identifying niches that align with your passions, interests, or areas of expertise. When you have a genuine interest in a niche, you'll be motivated to continually learn and create valuable content. Your passion will also come through in your promotions, making your recommendations more authentic and credible.

Demand and Profitability: Research the demand and profitability of potential niches. Look for niches with a significant audience and a proven track record of purchasing products or services. Use keyword research tools and online marketplaces to assess the search volume, competition, and potential profitability of keywords related to your niche.

Competition Analysis: Evaluate the level of competition within your chosen niches. High competition may indicate a thriving market, but it can be challenging to establish yourself. Look for niches where you can provide a unique value proposition or target a specific sub-niche with less competition. Finding a balance between demand and competition is essential for your success.

Affiliate Program Availability: Ensure that there are affiliate programs available within your chosen niche.

Look for reputable affiliate networks or individual merchants that offer products or services relevant to your niche. Assess commission structures, cookie durations, payment terms, and affiliate support. Choose affiliate programs that offer fair compensation and align with your audience's needs.

Target Audience: Understand the demographics, interests, and preferences of your target audience within the chosen niche. Identify their pain points, needs, and desires. This knowledge will help you tailor your content and promotions to resonate with your audience, increasing your chances of conversions and earning commissions.

Long-Term Viability: Consider the long-term viability of the niche. Evaluate whether it has the potential for sustained growth, evolving trends, and future opportunities. Avoid niches that are too narrow or have limited growth potential.

Aim for niches that offer scalability and room for expansion.

Evergreen vs. Trending Niches: Decide whether you prefer evergreen niches or trending niches. Evergreen niches are timeless and consistently in demand, such as health, personal finance, or self-improvement. Trending niches, on the other hand, capitalize on current trends or emerging industries. Both approaches have their advantages and disadvantages, so choose based on your interests and business goals.

Affiliate Marketing Compatibility: Consider the compatibility of the niche with affiliate marketing. Ensure that the products or services in the niche have affiliate programs available and offer reasonable commission rates. Some niches, such as digital products or software, often have higher commission rates compared to physical products.

Remember that selecting a profitable niche is just the first step. Once you've chosen a niche, conduct thorough market research, understand your audience, and develop effective marketing strategies. Continuously monitor and adapt your approach based on data and feedback from your audience. With the right combination of passion, market demand, and strategic planning, you can build a profitable affiliate marketing business within your chosen niche.

Researching and Evaluating Affiliate Programs

Researching and evaluating affiliate programs is a crucial step in affiliate marketing. The right affiliate programs can offer attractive commissions, quality products or services, reliable tracking, and excellent support. By conducting thorough research and evaluation, you can choose affiliate programs that align with your niche, audience, and business goals.

Here's a step-by-step guide on how to research and evaluate affiliate programs:

Define Your Criteria: Start by defining your criteria for evaluating affiliate programs. Consider factors such as commission structure, payment terms, cookie duration, product quality, affiliate support, and the reputation of the merchant or affiliate network.

Identifying your criteria will help you make consistent and objective evaluations.

Explore Affiliate Networks: Browse reputable affiliate networks such as ShareASale, CJ Affiliate, or ClickBank. These networks act as intermediaries between affiliates and merchants, offering a wide range of affiliate programs across various niches. Explore their directory or marketplace to discover programs that match your criteria and niche.

Niche-Specific Research: Conduct niche-specific research to identify affiliate programs directly offered by individual merchants. Look for merchants within your niche who have their own affiliate programs. Use search engines, social media, and industry-specific websites to find potential affiliate programs that may not be listed on affiliate networks.

Read Merchant Websites: Visit the websites of the merchants offering affiliate programs. Explore their product or service offerings, value proposition, customer testimonials, and overall branding. Assess the relevance and quality of their offerings to ensure they align with your niche and audience's needs.

Commission Structure and Payment Terms: Review the commission structure offered by the affiliate programs. Understand whether they provide a percentage-based commission or a fixed amount per sale or action. Evaluate the payment terms, such as payment frequency and minimum payout thresholds. Ensure that the commission rates and payment terms are fair and reasonable for your efforts.

Tracking and Reporting: Look for information about the tracking and reporting mechanisms provided by the affiliate programs.

Reliable tracking ensures that your referrals are properly attributed, and you receive accurate commission payments. Check if they offer access to real-time reporting, conversion tracking, and performance analytics to monitor your earnings and optimize your strategies.

Affiliate Support: Evaluate the level of support provided by the affiliate programs. Look for resources such as marketing materials, banners, product information, and dedicated affiliate managers. Responsive and helpful affiliate support can make a significant difference in your affiliate marketing journey, especially if you're new to the industry.

Merchant Reputation: Research the reputation of the merchant or affiliate network. Look for online reviews, testimonials, and feedback from other affiliates. Consider factors such as the merchant's track record, customer satisfaction, and ethical business practices.

A reputable merchant or network is more likely to provide a positive and trustworthy affiliate experience.

Consider Product or Service Quality: Assess the quality and relevance of the products or services offered by the affiliate programs. Look for products or services that are valuable, reputable, and align with your audience's needs. Promoting high-quality offerings enhances your credibility and increases the likelihood of conversions.

Evaluate Terms and Conditions: Carefully review the terms and conditions of the affiliate programs. Pay attention to any exclusions, restrictions, or promotional guidelines. Ensure that the terms and conditions are reasonable and align with your marketing strategies and ethical practices.

Seek Recommendations: Reach out to fellow affiliates, industry experts, or online communities within your niche. Seek recommendations for reliable and successful affiliate programs. Networking with experienced affiliates can provide valuable insights and save you time in finding reputable programs.

Compare and Make a Decision: After conducting thorough research and evaluation, compare the affiliate programs based on your defined criteria. Consider the pros and cons of each program, taking into account factors such as commission rates, product quality, support, and reputation. Make an informed decision based on the overall fit with your niche, audience, and business goals.

Remember that affiliate programs can evolve over time, so it's essential to periodically reassess their performance and relevance to your business.

By researching and evaluating affiliate programs diligently, you can choose partnerships that offer long-term value, maximize your earnings potential, and contribute to the success of your affiliate marketing endeavors.

Assessing Commission Structures and Payout Methods

When evaluating affiliate programs, one crucial aspect to consider is the commission structure and payout methods. The commission structure determines how affiliates are compensated for their promotional efforts, while the payout methods determine how affiliates receive their earnings. Understanding and assessing these aspects is vital to ensure that your affiliate marketing efforts are financially rewarding. ***Here's a guide on how to assess commission structures and payout methods***:

Commission Structure Variations: Familiarize yourself with the different types of commission structures commonly used in affiliate marketing. The most prevalent ones include:

a. Percentage-based Commission: Affiliates earn a percentage of the total sale amount or the referred customer's purchase value. This structure is popular and provides a scalable income potential.

b. Fixed Amount per Sale: Affiliates receive a fixed commission for every successful referral that leads to a sale. This structure is straightforward and guarantees a consistent payout per conversion.

c. Hybrid Commission: Some affiliate programs combine both a percentage-based commission and a fixed amount per sale. This hybrid structure can offer a competitive edge and provide flexibility in earnings.

Commission Rates: Evaluate the commission rates offered by affiliate programs. Compare the rates within your niche and consider whether they are competitive and aligned with your expectations. Look for programs that offer fair and attractive commission rates, keeping in mind that higher rates may not always equate to better profitability if the product prices are lower or conversion rates are low.

Multi-Tier Commissions: Some affiliate programs offer multi-tier commissions, which allow you to earn additional commissions by referring other affiliates to the program. Assess whether the program provides multi-tier commission

opportunities and determine if it aligns
with your business goals and networking
capabilities.

Payout Methods: Evaluate the payout
methods offered by affiliate programs.
Common payout methods include:

a. PayPal: PayPal is a widely used and
convenient payment method that allows
for quick and secure transactions. Check if
the affiliate program supports PayPal
payments and if there are any associated
fees or minimum payout thresholds.

b. Bank Transfer: Bank transfers provide
a direct deposit of funds into your bank
account. Determine if the affiliate program
offers bank transfers as a payout method
and consider any associated fees or
minimum payout thresholds.

c. Check: Some affiliate programs offer
payment via physical checks. Consider
whether this method is convenient for you,

taking into account potential delays in receiving the checks and any associated fees for check processing or international delivery.

d. Gift Cards or Store Credit: Certain affiliate programs may offer payout options in the form of gift cards or store credit. Assess whether these options align with your preferences and if there are limitations on where the gift cards can be used.

Payout Thresholds: Determine if the affiliate program has a minimum payout threshold, which is the minimum amount of earnings required before you can request a payout. Consider whether the threshold is reasonable and achievable based on your anticipated earnings and promotional efforts.

Payment Frequency: Evaluate the payment frequency offered by the affiliate program.

Some programs pay on a monthly basis, while others may have more frequent or less frequent payment schedules. Choose a program with a payment frequency that suits your financial needs and preferences.

Payment Stability and Reliability: Research the reputation and track record of the affiliate program regarding payment stability and reliability. Look for reviews and feedback from other affiliates to assess if the program consistently meets its payment obligations and if there have been any issues or delays in the past.

Currency and Exchange Rates: If you operate in a different currency than the affiliate program's default currency, consider the impact of exchange rates and any associated fees. Evaluate whether the program offers currency conversion options or if there are any costs involved in converting payments.

When assessing commission structures
and payout methods, it's essential to strike
a balance between attractive commission
rates and reliable payment methods. Look
for programs that offer competitive
commissions, convenient payout options,
reasonable payout thresholds, and a solid
reputation for timely payments. By
carefully evaluating these aspects, you can
select affiliate programs that align with
your financial goals and ensure a smooth
and rewarding affiliate marketing
experience.

Understanding Program Terms and Conditions

Understanding the terms and conditions of affiliate programs is essential for affiliate marketers. These terms and conditions outline the rules, obligations, and restrictions associated with participating in an affiliate program. Familiarizing yourself with these terms ensures that you comply with program requirements, maintain a positive relationship with merchants or affiliate networks, and protect your interests as an affiliate marketer. ***Here's a guide on how to understand program terms and conditions***:

Read the Terms and Conditions: Start by thoroughly reading the terms and conditions provided by the affiliate program. This document may be available on the merchant's website or within the affiliate network's platform. Pay close attention to all sections, including general provisions, affiliate responsibilities, payment terms, promotional guidelines, and termination clauses.

Affiliate Eligibility: Understand the eligibility criteria outlined in the terms and conditions. Check if there are any restrictions based on geographic location, age, or other factors. Ensure that you meet all eligibility requirements before joining the program to avoid any issues later on.

Commission Structure and Earnings: Review the commission structure and understand how your earnings will be calculated. Note the specific actions or conversions that qualify for commission payments. Determine if there are any limitations, such as exclusions for certain product categories or customer actions.

Cookie Duration: Pay attention to the cookie duration mentioned in the terms and conditions.

The cookie duration determines how long a referral will be tracked and attributed to your affiliate account. Longer cookie durations generally provide a higher chance of earning commissions for subsequent purchases made by referred customers within the specified timeframe.

Promotional Guidelines: Understand the promotional guidelines provided by the program. These guidelines may outline the permitted promotional methods, content restrictions, and branding requirements. Ensure that your marketing activities align with the guidelines to avoid any potential violations or disputes.

Prohibited Activities: Take note of any prohibited activities mentioned in the terms and conditions. These may include actions such as spamming, trademark infringement, or engaging in unethical practices. Complying with these guidelines is crucial to maintain a positive reputation as an affiliate marketer and avoid penalties or account suspension.

PPC Advertising and Keyword Usage: If you plan to engage in pay-per-click (PPC) advertising or use keywords related to the merchant's brand, understand any specific guidelines or restrictions outlined in the terms and conditions. Some programs may have limitations on bidding on certain keywords or using trademarked terms in your ads.

Tracking and Reporting: Familiarize yourself with the tracking and reporting mechanisms provided by the program. Understand how referrals are tracked, how conversions are attributed, and how you can access performance reports. This knowledge will help you monitor your progress, analyze campaign effectiveness, and optimize your affiliate marketing strategies.

Termination and Modification: Pay attention to the termination and modification clauses in the terms and conditions. Understand the conditions under which the program can terminate your affiliate account or modify the program's terms. Being aware of these provisions will help you protect your interests and adapt to any changes that may arise.

Support and Communication: Take note of the channels through which you can seek support or communicate with the program's administrators. This may include contact information for affiliate managers, support tickets, or dedicated affiliate forums. Understanding how to reach out for assistance will help you address any questions or concerns that may arise during your affiliate marketing journey.

Agreement Acceptance: Ensure that you explicitly accept the terms and conditions of the program. This acceptance is typically done by ticking a box or clicking a button during the signup process. By accepting the terms, you acknowledge your commitment to comply with the program's requirements.

If you have any questions or uncertainties regarding the terms and conditions, consider reaching out to the program's support team for clarification. It's crucial to have a clear understanding of the program's rules and expectations before you begin promoting their products or services. By understanding and adhering to the terms and conditions, you can build a strong and compliant affiliate marketing business.

Creating a Professional Website or Blog

Having a professional website or blog is crucial for affiliate marketers. It serves as the foundation of your online presence and acts as a platform to promote affiliate products or services effectively. A well-designed and user-friendly website can attract visitors, build trust, and increase the likelihood of conversions. *Here's a guide on how to create a professional website or blog for your affiliate marketing business*:

Choose a Domain Name: Select a domain name that is relevant to your niche and easy to remember. Ideally, it should be short, descriptive, and brandable. Consider using keywords related to your niche to improve search engine visibility.

Register your domain name with a reputable domain registrar.

Select a Web Hosting Provider: Choose a reliable web hosting provider that offers good server uptime, fast loading speeds, and excellent customer support. Consider your website's needs, such as the expected traffic volume and any specific technical requirements, when selecting a hosting plan.

Decide on a Content Management System (CMS): Select a content management system that suits your needs and technical expertise. Popular CMS options include WordPress, Joomla, and Drupal. WordPress is widely used and user-friendly, making it a popular choice for affiliate marketers.

Design and Layout: Opt for a professional and visually appealing design for your website. Select a clean and responsive theme that enhances user experience across various devices. Customize the layout, color scheme, and typography to match your branding and create a cohesive look.

Create High-Quality Content: Focus on creating valuable and engaging content that resonates with your target audience. Craft informative blog posts, product reviews, tutorials, or guides that provide solutions to your audience's problems or address their needs. Use high-quality images, videos, and graphics to enhance the visual appeal of your content.

Implement SEO Strategies: Optimize your website for search engines to increase its visibility in organic search results. Research and incorporate relevant keywords into your content, meta tags, and headings. Create descriptive and compelling meta titles and descriptions to encourage click-throughs from search engine users.

Integrate Affiliate Links: Strategically place affiliate links within your content to promote products or services. Ensure that the placement is natural and relevant to the context. Use a variety of link formats, such as text links, image links, or call-to-action buttons, to increase click-through rates.

Build a User-Friendly Navigation: Create a user-friendly navigation menu that allows visitors to easily explore your website and find the information they need. Organize your content into logical categories and use clear labels for menu items. Include a search bar to facilitate quick content discovery.

Optimize for Mobile Devices: With the increasing use of mobile devices, ensure that your website is mobile-friendly and responsive. Optimize your design and layout to adapt to different screen sizes, providing a seamless browsing experience for mobile users.

Implement Tracking and Analytics: Integrate tracking tools such as Google Analytics to monitor your website's performance. Analyze visitor behavior, traffic sources, and conversion rates to gain insights into the effectiveness of your affiliate marketing strategies. Use this data to make informed decisions and optimize your website's performance.

Incorporate Contact and About Pages: Include a contact page with your email address or contact form to encourage communication with your visitors. Create an About page that introduces yourself and explains your expertise in your niche. Building trust and credibility can positively impact your affiliate marketing efforts.

Provide Clear Call-to-Actions: Place clear and compelling call-to-action buttons or links strategically throughout your website.

Encourage visitors to take desired actions, such as making a purchase, signing up for a newsletter, or downloading a resource.

Ensure Fast Loading Speed: Optimize your website's loading speed to provide a smooth browsing experience. Compress images, minify CSS and JavaScript files, and leverage caching techniques to reduce loading times. A fast website improves user satisfaction and reduces bounce rates.

Implement Security Measures: Protect your website and your visitors' data by implementing security measures. Install an SSL certificate to enable secure browsing and encrypt sensitive information. Keep your CMS, themes, and plugins updated to minimize vulnerabilities.

Regularly Update and Maintain: Regularly update your website with fresh content, new affiliate offers, and relevant information.

Ensure that all links are working correctly and fix any broken links promptly. Regular maintenance helps to provide a positive user experience and ensures your website remains functional and up-to-date.

Remember, creating a professional website or blog is an ongoing process. Continuously refine and improve your website based on user feedback, analytics data, and emerging industry trends. By investing time and effort into creating a professional online presence, you can establish yourself as a trusted affiliate marketer and maximize your chances of success.

Optimizing Your Website for Search Engines

Search engine optimization (SEO) is crucial for affiliate marketers as it helps improve your website's visibility in search engine results and drives organic traffic to your site. By optimizing your website for search engines, you can increase the chances of attracting relevant visitors and potential customers. ***Here's a guide on how to optimize your website for search engines***:

Conduct Keyword Research: Start by researching relevant keywords related to your niche. Use keyword research tools to identify popular search terms with moderate competition. Focus on long-tail keywords that are specific and have higher chances of conversion. Incorporate these keywords naturally into your content, headings, meta tags, and image alt tags.

Optimize On-Page Elements: Pay attention to on-page elements that impact your website's search engine visibility:

Meta Titles and Descriptions: Craft unique and compelling meta titles and descriptions for each page. Include relevant keywords and provide a clear and concise description of the page's content.

Heading Tags: Use heading tags (H1, H2, H3, etc.) to structure your content and highlight important sections. Include relevant keywords in your headings to signal the page's topic to search engines.

URL Structure: Ensure your URLs are descriptive, concise, and include keywords when possible. Avoid using long strings of numbers or irrelevant characters in your URLs.

Image Optimization: Optimize your images by using descriptive file names and adding alt tags that describe the image.

This helps search engines understand the content of your images and can improve visibility in image search results.

Create High-Quality Content: Develop high-quality, informative, and engaging content that provides value to your target audience. Aim for comprehensive, well-researched articles, blog posts, and product reviews. Incorporate relevant keywords naturally within the content, but prioritize creating content that is reader-friendly and offers a great user experience.

Improve Website Speed: Page loading speed is an important factor in SEO. Optimize your website's speed by compressing images, minifying CSS and JavaScript files, enabling caching, and using a reliable hosting provider. A faster website improves user experience and increases the likelihood of higher search engine rankings.

Build Quality Backlinks: Earn high-quality backlinks from reputable websites in your niche. Focus on acquiring natural backlinks through content that others find valuable and share-worthy. Seek opportunities for guest blogging, participate in relevant forums or communities, and reach out to influencers or industry experts for potential collaborations.

Enhance User Experience: User experience plays a significant role in SEO. Ensure your website is user-friendly and easy to navigate. Improve site architecture, provide clear calls-to-action, optimize for mobile devices, and ensure that your website is accessible to users with disabilities. Positive user experience signals to search engines that your site is valuable and relevant.

Monitor Website Analytics: Set up website analytics tools like Google Analytics to track important metrics.

Monitor key data such as organic traffic, bounce rates, average session duration, and conversion rates. Analyze this data to identify areas for improvement and refine your SEO strategies accordingly.

Stay Updated with SEO Trends: SEO best practices and algorithms evolve over time. Stay updated with the latest SEO trends, algorithm updates, and industry news. Follow reputable SEO blogs, attend webinars, and participate in online communities to stay informed and adapt your SEO strategies accordingly.

Remember, SEO is a continuous process, and it may take time to see significant results. Be patient, consistently optimize your website, create valuable content, and focus on providing an exceptional user experience. By implementing effective SEO techniques, you can enhance your website's visibility, attract organic traffic, and ultimately increase your affiliate marketing success.

Utilizing Social Media Platforms for Promotion

Social media platforms provide excellent opportunities for affiliate marketers to promote their products or services, engage with their target audience, and drive traffic to their websites. By effectively utilizing social media platforms, you can expand your reach, increase brand awareness, and ultimately boost your affiliate marketing success. ***Here's a guide on how to leverage social media for promotion***:

Choose Relevant Social Media Platforms: Identify the social media platforms that align with your target audience and niche. Popular options include Facebook, Instagram, Twitter, LinkedIn, Pinterest, and YouTube. Consider the nature of your content and the type of engagement you want to foster to determine the most suitable platforms for your affiliate marketing business.

Optimize Your Social Media Profiles: Create compelling and professional profiles on each platform you choose. Use consistent branding elements such as your logo, color scheme, and bio information. Include relevant keywords and a clear description of what you offer. Add a link to your website or blog in your bio to drive traffic to your affiliate content.

Develop a Content Strategy: Plan your social media content strategically to engage your audience and promote your affiliate products or services effectively. Create a content calendar and decide on the type of content you will share, such as blog posts, product reviews, tutorials, videos, infographics, or promotional offers. Focus on providing valuable and relevant content that resonates with your audience.

Build and Nurture Your Social Media Community: Engage with your followers, respond to comments and messages, and foster a sense of community on your social media profiles. Encourage conversations, ask questions, and actively participate in discussions related to your niche. Building a loyal and engaged community can amplify the reach of your affiliate promotions and generate more interest in your content.

Share Engaging Visual Content: Utilize visual content, such as images, videos, and infographics, to capture attention and generate interest. High-quality visuals can significantly enhance engagement on social media. Create visually appealing content that showcases the benefits of the affiliate products or services you promote.

Use Affiliate Links Strategically: Incorporate affiliate links within your social media posts and updates. Ensure that the placement feels natural and non-intrusive. Use URL shorteners or custom tracking links provided by your affiliate network to track the performance of your social media promotions.

Leverage Influencer Marketing: Collaborate with influencers in your niche to expand your reach and tap into their existing audience. Seek out influencers who align with your brand and have an engaged following. Partner with them for product reviews, sponsored posts, or joint content collaborations to leverage their influence and drive traffic to your affiliate links.

Run Contests and Giveaways: Organize contests or giveaways on your social media platforms to incentivize engagement and increase brand awareness. Encourage participants to share your content, follow your page, or tag their friends to enter the contest. Offer prizes that are relevant to your niche or affiliate products to attract your target audience.

Engage in Social Listening: Monitor social media platforms for mentions of your brand, affiliate products, or relevant keywords related to your niche. Engage in conversations, offer assistance, and provide value whenever possible. Social listening helps you understand your audience's needs, address their concerns, and build relationships.

Analyze and Optimize: Utilize social media analytics tools provided by the platforms or third-party tools to track the performance of your social media efforts. Analyze engagement metrics, click-through rates, and conversion rates to determine the effectiveness of your promotions. Use this data to refine your social media strategies, identify successful tactics, and make informed decisions for future campaigns.

Stay Updated with Social Media Trends: Social media platforms are constantly evolving, introducing new features, and changing algorithms. Stay updated with the latest trends, algorithm updates, and best practices in social media marketing. Experiment with new features, leverage video content, explore live streaming options, and adapt your strategies accordingly.

Remember, building a strong social media presence takes time and consistent effort. Be authentic, provide value, and engage with your audience genuinely. By effectively utilizing social media platforms, you can create brand awareness, drive traffic to your affiliate content, and increase your chances of affiliate marketing success.

Chapter 5: Content Creation Strategies

Developing a Content Strategy

A well-planned content strategy is essential for successful affiliate marketing. It helps you create valuable, engaging, and relevant content that attracts and retains your target audience. By developing a content strategy, you can effectively promote your affiliate products or services, establish your expertise, and drive conversions. *Here's a step-by-step guide on how to develop a content strategy for your affiliate marketing business*:

Define Your Target Audience: Clearly identify your target audience and understand their needs, preferences, and pain points. Determine the demographics, interests, and behaviors of your audience to create content that resonates with them.

Set Clear Goals: Define your goals for your content strategy. Are you aiming to drive more traffic, increase conversions, build brand awareness, or educate your audience? Setting clear goals will help you shape your content and measure its success.

Identify Your Unique Selling Proposition: Determine what sets you apart from other affiliate marketers in your niche. Identify your unique selling proposition (USP) and leverage it in your content. Whether it's your expertise, personal experience, or a particular approach, highlight your USP to attract and connect with your audience.

Research Your Niche: Conduct thorough research within your niche to identify popular topics, trending issues, and gaps in existing content. Use keyword research tools, monitor industry forums, follow influencers, and engage with your target audience to gain insights into their interests and concerns.

Brainstorm Content Ideas: Based on your research, brainstorm content ideas that align with your audience's interests and address their needs. Generate a mix of content types, such as informative blog posts, product reviews, tutorials, case studies, videos, infographics, or podcasts. Aim for a variety of content formats to cater to different preferences and enhance engagement.

Plan a Content Calendar: Develop a content calendar to organize and schedule your content creation and publishing. Outline topics, keywords, and tentative publishing dates for each piece of content. This helps ensure a consistent flow of content and allows you to align it with relevant events, holidays, or product launches.

Create Valuable and Engaging Content: Focus on creating high-quality content that provides value to your audience. Offer insights, solve problems, answer questions, and educate your audience. Use a conversational tone, storytelling techniques, and engaging visuals to make your content more compelling and shareable.

Incorporate Affiliate Promotions: Integrate your affiliate promotions naturally within your content. Ensure that your affiliate links and product recommendations are relevant and add value to your audience. Avoid being overly promotional and prioritize providing genuine recommendations based on your expertise and experience.

Optimize for Search Engines: Incorporate SEO best practices into your content. Conduct keyword research to identify relevant keywords and phrases related to your content.

Optimize your titles, headings, meta tags, and image alt tags with keywords to improve search engine visibility.

Promote Your Content: Develop a promotional strategy to ensure your content reaches your target audience. Share your content on social media platforms, engage in relevant online communities and forums, collaborate with influencers, and leverage email marketing to drive traffic to your content.

Monitor and Analyze Performance: Regularly track the performance of your content using analytics tools. Analyze metrics such as page views, time on page, bounce rates, social shares, and conversions. This data will help you identify successful content types, understand your audience's preferences, and refine your content strategy.

Adapt and Evolve: Continuously evaluate the performance of your content strategy and make necessary adjustments. Stay updated with industry trends, listen to your audience's feedback, and experiment with new content formats or distribution channels to optimize your strategy over time.

Remember, consistency and quality are key to an effective content strategy. Focus on creating valuable, relevant, and engaging content that establishes your authority and builds trust with your audience. By aligning your content with their needs and interests, you can increase your affiliate marketing success and drive conversions.

Creating High-Quality and Engaging Content

Creating high-quality and engaging content is crucial for capturing the attention of your audience, establishing your authority, and driving conversions as an affiliate marketer. By focusing on quality, relevance, and engagement, you can provide value to your audience and increase the effectiveness of your affiliate promotions. ***Here are some tips on how to create high-quality and engaging content***:

Understand Your Audience: Gain a deep understanding of your target audience—their demographics, interests, pain points, and aspirations. Use this knowledge to tailor your content to their needs and preferences.

Provide Valuable Information: Offer valuable information that solves problems, answers questions, or educates your audience. Share insights, industry knowledge, tips, and actionable advice that your audience can benefit from.

Be Original and Unique: Differentiate yourself by offering unique perspectives, personal experiences, or innovative ideas. Don't be afraid to take a fresh approach or challenge conventional thinking in your niche.

Use a Conversational Tone: Write in a conversational tone that resonates with your audience. Use clear, concise language and avoid jargon or technical terms that may alienate or confuse your readers.

Tell Stories: Incorporate storytelling techniques to make your content more relatable and engaging. Share personal anecdotes, case studies, or success stories that illustrate your points and captivate your audience.

Utilize Engaging Formats: Experiment with different content formats to keep your audience engaged. Consider using videos, infographics, podcasts, or interactive elements to present information in an appealing and accessible way.

Incorporate Visuals: Include high-quality visuals, such as images, charts, or diagrams, to enhance your content. Visuals not only make your content more appealing but also help convey complex information more effectively.

Make it Readable: Break up your content into smaller sections with subheadings, bullet points, and numbered lists. Use short paragraphs and concise sentences to improve readability and make your content more scannable.

Incorporate Relevant Examples: Support your points with real-life examples that your audience can relate to. Show how the concepts or strategies you discuss have worked in specific scenarios, providing practical value to your readers.

Include Call-to-Actions (CTAs): Guide your audience on the desired next steps by including clear and compelling CTAs. Encourage them to take action, such as subscribing to your newsletter, sharing your content, or exploring affiliate products through your links.

Optimize for Search Engines: Implement basic search engine optimization (SEO) practices to improve the discoverability of your content. Conduct keyword research, optimize your titles and meta descriptions, and structure your content in a way that search engines can easily understand.

Edit and Proofread: Take the time to edit and proofread your content before publishing. Ensure that your grammar, spelling, and punctuation are accurate. Well-edited content enhances your professionalism and credibility.

Encourage Engagement: Foster interaction with your audience by encouraging comments, questions, and discussions. Respond to comments promptly, address inquiries, and engage in meaningful conversations to build a sense of community.

Analyze and Iterate: Use analytics tools to track the performance of your content. Monitor metrics such as page views, time on page, social shares, and conversions. Analyze the data to identify patterns, understand what works well, and refine your content strategy accordingly.

Continuously Improve: Strive for continuous improvement by seeking feedback from your audience and staying updated with industry trends. Adapt your content strategy based on the feedback received and the evolving needs of your audience.

Remember, quality and engagement should be at the core of your content creation efforts. By consistently delivering valuable and engaging content, you can establish your authority, build trust with your audience, and increase the effectiveness of your affiliate marketing endeavors.

Incorporating SEO Techniques in Your Content

Search engine optimization (SEO) plays a crucial role in driving organic traffic to your website and increasing the visibility of your content. By incorporating SEO techniques into your content, you can improve your search engine rankings, attract more relevant visitors, and enhance the overall success of your affiliate marketing efforts. *Here are some key SEO techniques to consider when creating content*:

Keyword Research: Conduct thorough keyword research to identify relevant search terms and phrases that your target audience uses when looking for information related to your niche. Use keyword research tools to discover high-volume keywords with low competition. Incorporate these keywords naturally into your content to increase its visibility to search engines.

Optimize Page Titles and Meta Descriptions: Craft compelling and keyword-rich page titles and meta descriptions for each piece of content. These elements provide a concise summary of your content and appear in search engine results. Make them enticing to encourage click-throughs from search engine users.

Use Heading Tags: Organize your content using heading tags (H1, H2, H3, etc.) to create a hierarchical structure. Include relevant keywords in your headings to help search engines understand the structure and context of your content. This also improves readability for your audience.

Create High-Quality Content: Focus on creating high-quality, informative, and engaging content that provides value to your audience. Search engines prioritize content that is useful and relevant to users. Incorporate your target keywords naturally throughout your content, but avoid keyword stuffing, which can harm your rankings.

Optimize URL Structure: Create clean and descriptive URLs for your content. Use relevant keywords in the URL to provide search engines with additional context about your content. Avoid using complex, randomly generated URLs that are difficult for users and search engines to understand.

Optimize Image Alt Text: When using images in your content, optimize the alt text attribute to describe the image using relevant keywords. This helps search engines understand the content of the image and improves accessibility for visually impaired users.

Internal and External Linking: Incorporate internal links within your content to connect related pages on your website. This helps search engines navigate and understand the structure of your site. Additionally, include relevant external links to reputable sources that provide additional value and context to your content.

Mobile-Friendly Design: Ensure that your website and content are mobile-friendly.

With the increasing use of mobile devices for internet browsing, search engines prioritize mobile-friendly websites in their rankings. Use responsive design and optimize your content for different screen sizes and devices.

Page Load Speed: Optimize your website and content for fast page load speeds. Slow-loading pages can negatively impact user experience and search engine rankings. Compress images, minify CSS and JavaScript files, and leverage caching techniques to improve page load times.

User Experience (UX): Prioritize a positive user experience on your website. User-friendly navigation, clear and well-structured content, and easy-to-use interfaces contribute to a better user experience. Search engines consider user signals such as bounce rate and time spent on page as ranking factors.

Regularly Update and Refresh Content: Keep your content fresh and up to date. Search engines value recently updated content, and regularly refreshing your existing content can help improve its visibility. Review and update outdated information, add new insights, and ensure that your content remains relevant.

Track and Analyze Performance: Utilize analytics tools to track the performance of your content. Monitor important metrics such as organic traffic, keyword rankings, bounce rate, and conversions. Analyze the data to gain insights into the effectiveness of your SEO efforts and make informed decisions for optimization.

Remember, SEO is an ongoing process that requires continuous effort and adaptation. Stay updated with the latest SEO best practices, algorithm changes, and industry trends to ensure that your content remains optimized for search engines and delivers long-term organic traffic to your affiliate marketing website.

Exploring Various Traffic Generation Methods

As an affiliate marketer, generating consistent traffic to your website is essential for the success of your affiliate marketing efforts. By exploring various traffic generation methods, you can attract a steady stream of relevant visitors, increase your brand exposure, and maximize your affiliate conversions. *Here are some effective traffic generation methods to consider*:

Search Engine Optimization (SEO): Optimize your website and content for search engines to improve your organic rankings. Focus on keyword research, on-page optimization, quality content creation, and building authoritative backlinks to increase your visibility in search engine results.

Content Marketing: Create high-quality and valuable content that resonates with your target audience. Publish informative blog posts, guides, tutorials, or videos that address their needs and provide solutions. Promote your content through social media, email marketing, and guest posting to drive traffic back to your website.

Social Media Marketing: Leverage the power of social media platforms to expand your reach and engage with your audience. Establish a strong presence on platforms like Facebook, Instagram, Twitter, LinkedIn, or YouTube. Share your content, engage with your followers, run targeted ad campaigns, and utilize relevant hashtags to drive traffic to your website.

Pay-Per-Click (PPC) Advertising: Consider running PPC ad campaigns on platforms such as Google Ads, Bing Ads, or social media advertising networks. Create compelling ad copies, select relevant keywords, and set a budget to display your ads to a targeted audience. PPC advertising can help you generate immediate traffic to your website.

Email Marketing: Build an email list of subscribers who are interested in your niche. Provide valuable content and offers through email newsletters, automated drip campaigns, or targeted email sequences. Drive traffic to your website by including links to relevant content or affiliate product recommendations in your emails.

Influencer Marketing: Collaborate with influencers in your niche to tap into their established audience and credibility. Identify influencers whose audience aligns with your target market and work on partnerships or sponsored content to promote your website or affiliate products. Influencer endorsements can drive significant traffic and increase conversions.

Guest Blogging: Write informative and engaging guest posts for reputable blogs in your niche. Include a link back to your website in your author bio or within the content itself. Guest blogging helps you reach a wider audience, enhance your authority, and drive traffic from the guest blog's readership.

Video Marketing: Create engaging and informative videos related to your niche and publish them on platforms like YouTube or Vimeo. Optimize your video titles, descriptions, and tags with relevant keywords. Include links to your website or affiliate products in the video descriptions to drive traffic.

Forum Participation: Join online forums and communities related to your niche and actively engage with the members. Provide valuable insights, answer questions, and contribute to discussions. Include a link to your website in your forum signature or whenever relevant to attract interested users to your website.

Podcasting: Start your own podcast or be a guest on existing podcasts within your niche. Share valuable insights, interview industry experts, and promote your website or affiliate products during the podcast episodes. Include links in the podcast description to drive traffic to your website.

Webinars and Live Events: Host webinars, workshops, or live events where you can showcase your expertise and provide value to your audience. Promote these events through your website, social media, and email marketing to drive traffic and engage with potential customers.

Online Advertising: Explore online advertising options beyond PPC, such as banner ads, native advertising, or sponsored content placements on relevant websites or industry publications.

Target websites or platforms that attract your target audience to increase your website traffic.

Remember, traffic generation requires a combination of strategies tailored to your niche and target audience. Experiment with different methods, track your results, and refine your approach based on what works best for your affiliate marketing goals. Continuously analyze your traffic sources and adjust your strategies to ensure a consistent flow of relevant visitors to your website.

Search Engine Optimization (SEO) Techniques

Search engine optimization (SEO) techniques are crucial for improving the visibility and ranking of your website in search engine results pages. By implementing effective SEO strategies, you can attract organic traffic, increase your website's authority, and boost your affiliate marketing success. *Here are some essential SEO techniques to consider*:

Keyword Research: Conduct thorough keyword research to identify relevant keywords and phrases that your target audience uses when searching for information related to your niche. Use keyword research tools to find high-volume keywords with manageable competition. Incorporate these keywords naturally into your website's content, titles, headings, meta tags, and URLs.

On-Page Optimization: Optimize your website's on-page elements to make it more search engine-friendly. Ensure that each page has a unique and descriptive title tag, relevant meta description, and properly structured headings (H1, H2, etc.). Use keywords strategically throughout the content while maintaining readability and natural flow.

Quality Content Creation: Focus on creating high-quality, valuable, and engaging content that addresses the needs and interests of your target audience. Develop comprehensive blog posts, articles, guides, and product reviews that provide useful information. Use keywords naturally within the content and incorporate relevant multimedia elements such as images and videos.

Site Architecture and Internal Linking: Design a logical site architecture that allows search engines to crawl and index your website effectively. Create a clear navigation structure, use XML sitemaps, and optimize your URLs to be descriptive and user-friendly. Incorporate internal links between related pages on your site to improve navigation and enhance the user experience.

Mobile Optimization: Ensure that your website is fully optimized for mobile devices. With the increasing number of users accessing the internet through mobile devices, search engines prioritize mobile-friendly websites. Use responsive design, optimize page load speed, and ensure that your content is easily accessible and readable on mobile screens.

Link Building: Earn high-quality backlinks from reputable and relevant websites to improve your website's authority and search engine rankings. Focus on acquiring natural links through guest blogging, influencer collaborations, content promotion, and creating shareable content. Avoid spammy link-building practices that can negatively impact your website's credibility.

User Experience (UX): Create a positive user experience on your website to improve engagement and rankings. Ensure fast page load times, intuitive navigation, mobile responsiveness, and easy-to-use interfaces. Encourage user interaction, such as comments and social sharing, to signal to search engines that your website provides value to users.

Technical SEO: Pay attention to technical aspects that impact your website's performance and crawlability. Optimize your site's robots.txt file, XML sitemaps, and structured data markup. Fix broken links, optimize image sizes, and use canonical tags to prevent duplicate content issues. Regularly monitor and optimize your website's performance, including server response times and website security.

Social Signals: Engage with your audience on social media platforms and encourage social sharing of your content. While social signals may not directly impact search engine rankings, they can increase the visibility of your content, attract more visitors, and potentially lead to natural backlinks.

Continuous Monitoring and Analysis: Regularly monitor your website's performance using analytics tools. Track key metrics such as organic traffic, keyword rankings, bounce rate, and conversions. Analyze the data to identify areas for improvement, assess the effectiveness of your SEO strategies, and make data-driven decisions to optimize your website further.

Remember, SEO is an ongoing process that requires consistent effort and adaptation. Stay updated with the latest algorithm changes, industry trends, and best practices to maintain a competitive edge and improve your website's search engine visibility.

Paid Advertising Strategies

Paid advertising is an effective way to quickly generate traffic, increase brand visibility, and drive conversions for your affiliate marketing business. By utilizing paid advertising strategies, you can reach a targeted audience, maximize your marketing efforts, and achieve your affiliate marketing goals. Here are some popular paid advertising strategies to consider:

Pay-Per-Click (PPC) Advertising: PPC advertising allows you to display your ads on search engine results pages (SERPs) or other websites and pay only when someone clicks on your ad. Platforms such as Google Ads and Bing Ads enable you to create and manage PPC campaigns. Conduct keyword research, craft compelling ad copy, set bid amounts, and target specific demographics to reach your desired audience.

Display Advertising: Display advertising involves placing banner ads or visual ads on relevant websites or advertising networks. You can use platforms like Google Display Network or social media advertising platforms to target specific websites or demographic groups. Create visually appealing ads that attract attention and entice users to click through to your website or landing page.

Social Media Advertising: Social media platforms, such as Facebook, Instagram, Twitter, and LinkedIn, offer robust advertising options to reach your target audience. These platforms provide detailed targeting capabilities based on demographics, interests, behaviors, and more. Create engaging ad content, leverage visual elements, and use compelling calls-to-action to drive traffic and conversions.

Native Advertising: Native advertising involves blending your ads seamlessly within the content of a platform or website. Native ads are designed to match the style and format of the surrounding content, making them less intrusive and more likely to be viewed by users. Native ads can be effective in driving traffic and generating leads when done strategically and in alignment with the platform's guidelines.

Influencer Marketing: Collaborating with influencers in your niche can help you tap into their established audience and gain exposure for your affiliate products or services. Influencers can promote your offerings through sponsored posts, reviews, or endorsements. Partnering with relevant influencers can provide targeted visibility and boost conversions.

Remarketing: Remarketing allows you to target users who have previously visited your website or interacted with your content. By using platforms like Google Ads or Facebook Pixel, you can display customized ads to these users as they browse other websites or social media platforms. Remarketing helps to re-engage with interested users and increase the chances of conversion.

Affiliate Network Advertising: Some affiliate networks offer advertising opportunities within their platforms. You can advertise your affiliate products or services to a network's audience through banners, sponsored listings, or email newsletters. Take advantage of these advertising options to reach a relevant audience within the affiliate marketing ecosystem.

Video Advertising: Video advertising on platforms like YouTube or social media can be highly effective in capturing users' attention and conveying your message. Create engaging video content that showcases your products or services and includes a call-to-action to drive traffic and conversions.

Sponsored Content: Partner with relevant websites or influencers to have your content featured as sponsored content. This can include sponsored blog posts, articles, or videos that promote your affiliate products or provide valuable information to the target audience. Sponsored content can enhance brand visibility and drive targeted traffic to your website.

Affiliate Program Advertising: Promote your affiliate program through paid advertising to attract potential affiliates who can help promote your products or services. Use PPC advertising, display ads, or sponsored listings on affiliate marketing platforms to reach individuals interested in joining affiliate programs.

When implementing paid advertising strategies, it's important to set clear goals, closely monitor campaign performance, and regularly optimize your ads to maximize their effectiveness. Conduct thorough research, test different approaches, and analyze the results to refine your paid advertising strategies and achieve optimal return on investment (ROI).

Building an Email List of Subscribers

Building an email list of subscribers is a valuable asset for any affiliate marketer. It allows you to directly communicate with your audience, nurture relationships, and promote your affiliate products or services effectively. ***Here are some key steps to help you build an email list***:

Choose an Email Marketing Service: Select a reliable email marketing service provider that suits your needs. Popular options include Mailchimp, ConvertKit, AWeber, and GetResponse. These platforms offer features such as email automation, subscriber management, and campaign tracking.

Create an Opt-In Form: Design an opt-in form to capture visitor information on your website. Place the form strategically, such as in the sidebar, footer, or as a pop-up. Keep the form simple, asking for essential information like name and email address. Offer an incentive, such as a free e-book, checklist, or exclusive content, to encourage visitors to subscribe.

Craft Compelling Lead Magnets: Develop high-quality lead magnets that provide value to your target audience. This can be an e-book, video series, cheat sheet, or any other content relevant to your niche. Make sure the lead magnet is informative, solves a problem, or fulfills a need your audience has. Promote your lead magnet across your website and social media platforms to attract subscribers.

Offer Opt-In Incentives: In addition to lead magnets, consider offering other opt-in incentives to entice visitors to subscribe. This could include exclusive discounts, access to a members-only area, or early access to new content or product launches. These incentives provide additional value and increase the chances of visitors subscribing to your email list.

Use Landing Pages: Create dedicated landing pages that focus on promoting your lead magnets and collecting email addresses. Optimize these pages with compelling headlines, persuasive copy, and clear calls-to-action. A well-designed landing page can significantly increase conversion rates and help grow your email list.

Implement Content Upgrades: Content upgrades are additional resources or bonuses offered within your blog posts or content in exchange for an email subscription. For example, you can offer a downloadable PDF version of the blog post, a checklist, or a bonus video tutorial. Content upgrades provide extra value and encourage readers to subscribe to access the additional content.

Leverage Social Media: Promote your email list on social media platforms to reach a wider audience. Create engaging posts that highlight the benefits of subscribing to your email list and direct users to your opt-in form or landing page. Use compelling visuals, catchy headlines, and clear calls-to-action to capture their attention and encourage them to sign up.

Engage with Subscribers: Once subscribers join your email list, nurture the relationship by sending regular emails with valuable content. Share informative blog posts, exclusive offers, product updates, and helpful tips related to your niche. Encourage engagement by asking for feedback, conducting surveys, or providing opportunities for subscribers to interact with you.

Segment Your Email List: Segmenting your email list allows you to deliver targeted content to specific groups of subscribers based on their interests, preferences, or behaviors. This ensures that your emails are relevant and personalized, increasing engagement and conversions. Use the data collected during the signup process or through subsequent interactions to segment your list effectively.

Maintain GDPR Compliance: If your audience includes individuals from the European Union (EU), ensure that your email marketing practices comply with the General Data Protection Regulation (GDPR). Obtain explicit consent from EU subscribers, provide clear privacy policies, and offer an easy way to unsubscribe from your email list.

Building an email list is an ongoing process that requires continuous effort, content creation, and engagement. Regularly analyze your email marketing metrics, such as open rates, click-through rates, and conversions, to assess the effectiveness of your campaigns. Continually refine your strategies based on subscriber feedback and evolving industry best practices to maximize the benefits of your email list.

Crafting Effective Email Campaigns

Crafting effective email campaigns is essential for engaging your subscribers, building relationships, and driving conversions in your affiliate marketing endeavors.

__By following these key steps, you can create impactful and successful email campaigns__:

Define Your Campaign Goals: Clearly define the objectives of your email campaign. Is it to promote a specific product, announce a new offer, provide valuable content, or nurture relationships with your subscribers? Having a clear goal will guide your content creation and call-to-action.

Segment Your Email List: Segment your email list based on subscriber preferences, demographics, purchase history, or engagement level. This allows you to deliver more personalized and targeted content, resulting in higher open rates, click-through rates, and conversions.

Write Compelling Subject Lines: The subject line is the first impression your subscribers have of your email.

Craft concise, compelling subject lines that grab attention, generate curiosity, and entice recipients to open your email. Use personalization, urgency, or a clear benefit to increase open rates.

Personalize Your Emails:
Personalization goes beyond just including the subscriber's name. Use the data you have about your subscribers to create personalized content that resonates with their interests and needs. Segment-based personalization, such as referencing past purchases or preferences, helps build a stronger connection.

Create Engaging Content: Focus on creating valuable, relevant, and engaging content in your emails. Balance promotional content with educational or entertaining content to keep your subscribers interested. Use a conversational tone, tell stories, and include visuals to enhance the overall experience.

Use Clear and Compelling Calls-to-Action (CTAs): Every email should have a clear call-to-action that drives the desired action from your subscribers. Use actionable language, prominent buttons or links, and a sense of urgency to encourage clicks and conversions. Ensure your CTAs are relevant to the email content and align with your campaign goals.

Optimize for Mobile Devices: With the increasing use of mobile devices, it's crucial to optimize your email campaigns for mobile viewing. Ensure your emails are responsive, have a mobile-friendly layout, and are easy to read and navigate on small screens. Test your emails across different devices and email clients to ensure a seamless experience.

Test and Optimize: Continuously test different elements of your email campaigns to optimize their performance. Test variations of subject lines, CTAs, content formats, and sending times to identify what resonates best with your audience. Use A/B testing to compare different versions and make data-driven decisions for improvement.

Monitor and Analyze Metrics: Regularly monitor and analyze key email marketing metrics such as open rates, click-through rates, conversion rates, and unsubscribe rates. These metrics provide insights into the effectiveness of your campaigns and help you identify areas for improvement. Leverage analytics tools provided by your email marketing service to gain valuable insights.

Maintain Consistency and Frequency: Maintain a consistent schedule for sending your emails to keep your subscribers engaged. Whether it's a weekly newsletter, monthly updates, or automated sequences, consistency is key. However, ensure that you don't overwhelm your subscribers with excessive emails. Find a frequency that strikes the right balance and aligns with your audience's expectations.

Monitor Deliverability and Compliance: Pay attention to email deliverability to ensure that your emails land in your subscribers' inboxes. Follow email best practices, manage your sender reputation, and adhere to anti-spam regulations. Regularly clean your email list to remove inactive or non-engaging subscribers to maintain a healthy list.

Seek Subscriber Feedback: Encourage feedback from your subscribers to understand their preferences, needs, and expectations better. Include surveys, feedback forms, or reply options in your emails. Act on the feedback received to improve your future email campaigns and strengthen your relationship with subscribers.

Crafting effective email campaigns requires a blend of creativity, data analysis, and understanding your audience. Continuously refine your strategies, experiment with different approaches, and learn from the results to optimize your email marketing efforts and drive success in your affiliate marketing business.

Automating Email Sequences for Affiliate Promotions

Automating email sequences for affiliate promotions can significantly enhance your efficiency and effectiveness as an affiliate marketer. With automated email sequences, you can deliver targeted and timely content to your subscribers, promote affiliate products or services, and nurture relationships on autopilot. *Here's how to effectively automate your email sequences for affiliate promotions*:

Set Clear Campaign Objectives: Define the goals of your email sequence. Determine what specific affiliate products or services you want to promote and the desired outcomes, such as driving conversions, increasing click-through rates, or educating subscribers. Clear objectives will guide your content creation and automation strategy.

Choose an Email Marketing Platform: Select a reputable email marketing platform that offers automation features. Popular platforms like Mailchimp, ConvertKit, or ActiveCampaign provide robust automation capabilities, including email triggers, segmentation, and drip campaigns. Ensure the platform integrates with your affiliate marketing tools and offers the necessary customization options.

Segment Your Email List: Segment your email list based on subscriber preferences, engagement level, or previous interactions. This allows you to deliver more personalized content and promotions to specific segments of your audience. Segmenting enables you to tailor your affiliate promotions to the interests and needs of different subscriber groups, increasing the chances of engagement and conversions.

Create a Drip Campaign: A drip campaign is a series of automated emails sent over a predefined schedule or triggered by specific subscriber actions. Plan a sequence of emails that gradually introduces your affiliate product or service, highlights its benefits, addresses common objections, and encourages action. Design the sequence to provide value and build anticipation as the promotion unfolds.

Write Compelling Email Content: Craft engaging and persuasive email content for each step of your automated sequence. Use attention-grabbing subject lines, captivating introductions, and persuasive calls-to-action. Clearly communicate the value proposition of the affiliate product or service and address how it can solve the subscriber's pain points or fulfill their needs. Balance promotional content with useful information to maintain a strong relationship with your audience.

Use Behavioral Triggers: Implement behavioral triggers to automate email sequences based on specific actions or events. For example, you can set up triggers for when a subscriber clicks a particular link, completes a purchase, or joins a specific segment. These triggers allow you to send targeted follow-up emails, cross-promotions, or personalized offers based on the subscriber's behavior, increasing relevance and engagement.

Leverage Dynamic Content: Dynamic content allows you to personalize emails based on subscriber attributes or preferences. Incorporate dynamic content in your automated sequences to create a more tailored experience for your subscribers. Customize product recommendations, greetings, or relevant content based on data like purchase history, geographic location, or demographic information.

Test and Optimize: Continuously monitor and analyze the performance of your automated email sequences. Test different elements, such as subject lines, email copy, call-to-action placement, and sending times, to optimize engagement and conversions. A/B testing can help you identify the most effective variations and make data-driven improvements.

Provide Value Beyond Promotion:
While the primary goal of your automated
sequence is to promote affiliate products
or services, it's essential to provide value
beyond promotion. Include helpful tips,
educational content, or exclusive resources
that align with your audience's interests.
This approach fosters trust and strengthens
your relationship with subscribers,
increasing the likelihood of engagement
and conversions.

Monitor Metrics and Refine: Regularly
analyze key email marketing metrics, such
as open rates, click-through rates,
conversion rates, and unsubscribe rates.
Assess the effectiveness of your
automated sequences, identify areas for
improvement, and make data-backed
adjustments. Use the insights gained to
refine your email content, sequence flow,
or segment targeting for better results.

Comply with Email Regulations: Ensure that your automated email sequences comply with relevant email marketing regulations, such as the CAN-SPAM Act or GDPR. Include unsubscribe options, provide clear privacy policies, and honor subscriber preferences. Maintain good sender reputation and avoid spammy practices to ensure deliverability and maintain a positive relationship with your subscribers.

Automating your email sequences for affiliate promotions saves you time, allows for personalized communication, and maximizes the impact of your affiliate marketing efforts. By providing valuable content, targeting specific segments, and continuously optimizing your sequences, you can drive engagement, conversions, and long-term success as an affiliate marketer.

Building Relationships with Your Audience

Building strong relationships with your audience is a crucial aspect of successful affiliate marketing. By establishing trust, fostering engagement, and providing value, you can create a loyal and supportive community. ***Here are some key strategies to build relationships with your audience***:

Know Your Target Audience:
Understand your target audience's needs, preferences, and pain points. Conduct market research, analyze demographics, and engage in conversations with your audience to gain insights. This knowledge enables you to tailor your content and affiliate promotions to their specific interests and challenges.

Be Authentic and Transparent: Authenticity is vital in building relationships. Be genuine in your communication, voice your opinions, and share your experiences. Transparency builds trust, so be open about your affiliations and disclose any financial interests. Authenticity and transparency create a sense of credibility and help you connect on a deeper level with your audience.

Engage in Two-Way Communication: Encourage dialogue and foster interaction with your audience. Respond to comments, messages, and emails in a timely and meaningful manner. Actively participate in social media discussions, forums, and online communities related to your niche. Show genuine interest in your audience's feedback, questions, and concerns to strengthen the connection.

Provide Valuable Content: Consistently deliver high-quality, valuable content that meets your audience's needs. Offer solutions to their problems, share actionable tips, and provide relevant information. Create a mix of formats such as blog posts, videos, podcasts, or social media posts to cater to different preferences. Valuable content establishes you as a trusted authority and keeps your audience engaged.

Personalize Your Communication: Treat your audience as individuals by personalizing your communication. Use their names in emails or messages and segment your email list to deliver targeted content. Tailor your promotions based on their preferences or past interactions. Personalization enhances the sense of connection and demonstrates that you understand and value your audience's unique needs.

Effective Communication and Engagement Strategies

Effective communication and engagement strategies are crucial for affiliate marketers to connect with their audience, build relationships, and drive conversions. By employing these strategies, you can ensure your messages are well-received, encourage active participation, and foster a loyal and engaged community. *Here are some key strategies for effective communication and engagement*:

Clear and Concise Messaging: Communicate your message in a clear and concise manner. Avoid jargon or complex language that may confuse your audience. Use simple, easy-to-understand language that resonates with your target audience. Craft compelling headlines and subject lines that grab attention and convey the value of your content or promotions.

Active Listening: Actively listen to your audience by paying attention to their feedback, comments, and questions. Take the time to understand their needs, preferences, and concerns. Show empathy and respond genuinely to their inquiries. This practice demonstrates that you value their opinions and are committed to meeting their needs.

Use Multiple Communication Channels: Utilize a variety of communication channels to reach your audience effectively. This may include your website or blog, social media platforms, email newsletters, podcasts, videos, or webinars. Different channels cater to different preferences, allowing you to engage with a wider audience. Adapt your communication style to each platform while maintaining a consistent brand voice.

Personalize Communication: Personalization is key to establishing a connection with your audience. Address individuals by their names when possible and use segmentation to deliver targeted content. Tailor your messages to their interests, preferences, or previous interactions. This level of personalization shows that you understand their unique needs and enhances engagement.

Encourage Two-Way Communication: Foster an environment of dialogue and encourage your audience to participate. Prompt them to leave comments, ask questions, or share their experiences. Respond to their inquiries promptly and thoughtfully. Engage in conversations on social media platforms or within online communities related to your niche. By encouraging two-way communication, you create a sense of community and build stronger relationships.

Provide Valuable Content: Offer high-quality, valuable content that meets the needs of your audience. Create informative blog posts, tutorials, guides, or videos that address their pain points and offer practical solutions. Share industry insights, tips, or case studies that demonstrate your expertise. Valuable content establishes you as a trusted source of information, encouraging your audience to engage and share your content with others.

Incorporate Visuals: Visual content is highly engaging and helps convey messages more effectively. Use relevant images, infographics, videos, or slide presentations to enhance your communication. Visuals not only capture attention but also make information more digestible and shareable. They can evoke emotions, tell stories, and leave a lasting impression on your audience.

Run Contests or Giveaways: Organize contests or giveaways to encourage active participation from your audience. This can be done through social media platforms or email campaigns. Offer enticing prizes related to your niche to incentivize engagement. Contests and giveaways generate excitement, increase brand visibility, and attract new followers or subscribers.

Collaborate with Influencers: Partnering with influencers in your niche can expand your reach and enhance engagement. Identify relevant influencers with an engaged audience and establish mutually beneficial collaborations. This may include guest posting on their blogs, hosting joint webinars or live events, or featuring them in your content. Influencers can introduce you to their audience, providing an opportunity to engage with new potential customers.

Analyze and Adjust: Regularly analyze engagement metrics and feedback to assess the effectiveness of your communication strategies. Monitor metrics such as open rates, click-through rates, comments, shares, or conversions. Identify what resonates with your audience and adjust your communication strategies accordingly. Continuously refine your approach based on data-driven insights.

Effective communication and engagement strategies are essential for affiliate marketers to establish a strong connection with their audience, foster loyalty, and drive conversions. By delivering valuable content, listening actively, personalizing communication, and leveraging multiple channels, you can create a vibrant and engaged community that supports your affiliate marketing efforts.

Share Personal Stories: Share personal stories and experiences that resonate with your audience. This allows them to relate to you on a more personal level and builds a stronger bond. Stories create an emotional connection and help your audience see you as a relatable figure rather than just a marketer. Be vulnerable, share your successes and failures, and demonstrate how you've overcome challenges.

Encourage User-generated Content: Encourage your audience to create and share content related to your niche. This can include testimonials, reviews, or success stories. User-generated content not only strengthens your relationship with individual contributors but also serves as social proof for others in your audience. Highlight and engage with user-generated content to foster a sense of community and collaboration.

Be Consistent and Reliable: Consistency is key in building relationships. Consistently provide valuable content, engage with your audience, and maintain a regular presence across your communication channels. Be reliable in delivering what you promise, whether it's timely responses, consistent updates, or fulfilling commitments. Consistency and reliability build trust and confidence in your audience.

Offer Exclusive Benefits: Provide exclusive benefits or rewards to your loyal audience members. This could include access to premium content, early product launches, special discounts, or exclusive events. By offering unique perks, you make your audience feel appreciated and valued, further strengthening the relationship.

Seek Feedback and Act on It: Actively seek feedback from your audience to understand their needs, preferences, and areas for improvement. Conduct surveys, polls, or feedback forms to gather insights. Act on the feedback received, whether it's adjusting your content strategy, addressing concerns, or implementing suggestions. By demonstrating that you listen and respond to their feedback, you show your audience that their opinions matter.

Building relationships with your audience is an ongoing process that requires consistent effort, genuine interaction, and a focus on providing value. By fostering trust, engagement, and a sense of community, you can cultivate a loyal and supportive audience that not only engages with your affiliate promotions but also becomes brand advocates.

Utilizing Social Media for Audience Interaction

Social media platforms provide powerful tools for affiliate marketers to engage with their audience, build relationships, and promote their affiliate products or services. By utilizing social media effectively, you can create a thriving community, encourage interaction, and drive conversions. ***Here are some strategies for utilizing social media for audience interaction***:

Choose the Right Platforms: Select social media platforms that align with your target audience's demographics, interests, and preferences. Popular platforms such as Facebook, Instagram, Twitter, LinkedIn, and YouTube offer unique features and audience demographics. Focus on the platforms where your target audience is most active to maximize your engagement potential.

Create Compelling Profiles: Optimize your social media profiles to reflect your brand identity and attract your target audience. Use professional profile images, engaging cover photos, and descriptive bios. Include relevant keywords, hashtags, and a link to your website or blog. Craft a compelling and concise brand message that resonates with your audience.

Share Valuable Content: Consistently share valuable and relevant content that appeals to your audience. Create a mix of content formats, including blog posts, videos, infographics, or podcasts, to cater to different preferences. Share industry insights, educational tips, product reviews, or behind-the-scenes glimpses. Provide information that educates, entertains, or inspires your audience.

Encourage Engagement: Prompt your audience to engage with your social media posts by asking questions, inviting comments, or seeking opinions. Create polls, surveys, or quizzes to encourage participation. Respond to comments, messages, and mentions in a timely and personalized manner. Show genuine interest in your audience's thoughts and foster a sense of community.

Leverage Visual Content: Visual content is highly effective in capturing attention and driving engagement on social media. Use eye-catching images, videos, or graphics in your posts to make them more shareable and appealing. Incorporate visual storytelling techniques to evoke emotions and convey messages effectively.

Utilize Live Video: Take advantage of live video features on platforms like Facebook Live, Instagram Live, or YouTube Live. Hosting live Q&A sessions, product demonstrations, or behind-the-scenes glimpses can create a real-time connection with your audience. Interact with viewers, respond to their comments, and address their questions directly, fostering a sense of authenticity and immediacy.

Collaborate with Influencers: Partnering with influencers in your niche can expand your social media reach and boost engagement. Identify relevant influencers with a loyal and engaged following. Collaborate on joint content, cross-promotions, or sponsored posts to tap into their audience and increase your visibility. Influencers can bring fresh perspectives, credibility, and social proof to your affiliate promotions.

Use Hashtags Strategically: Incorporate relevant hashtags in your social media posts to increase discoverability and join relevant conversations. Research popular and trending hashtags in your niche and use them appropriately.

Engage with posts using relevant hashtags from other users, showing your support and expanding your reach beyond your existing audience.

Run Contests or Giveaways: Organize social media contests or giveaways to incentivize engagement and reward your audience. Encourage participants to like, comment, share, or tag others to enter the contest. Offer prizes that are relevant to your niche or affiliate products. Contests and giveaways generate excitement, attract new followers, and increase brand visibility.

Analyze Metrics and Adjust: Regularly analyze social media metrics, such as engagement rates, reach, clicks, or conversions, to evaluate the effectiveness of your strategies. Use social media analytics tools or platform insights to gain insights into your audience's behavior and preferences.

Adjust your content strategy, posting schedule, or engagement tactics based on data-driven insights.

Utilizing social media for audience interaction empowers you to connect with your target audience on a personal level, build trust, and drive engagement. By delivering valuable content, encouraging interaction, and leveraging the unique features of each platform, you can create a vibrant and engaged social media community that supports your affiliate marketing goals.

Chapter 9: Tracking and Analytics

Setting Up Tracking Tools and Software

Tracking tools and software play a crucial role in affiliate marketing, enabling you to monitor the performance of your campaigns, analyze data, and optimize your strategies for better results. By setting up tracking tools effectively, you can gain valuable insights into your affiliate marketing efforts and make informed decisions. *Here are the key steps to setting up tracking tools and software*:

Define Your Tracking Goals: Start by identifying your tracking goals. Determine the key metrics you want to measure, such as clicks, conversions, sales, or revenue. Clarify what data points are essential for evaluating the success of your affiliate campaigns. Clear tracking goals will guide your tool selection and configuration.

Select a Tracking Tool or Software: Research and choose a tracking tool or software that aligns with your needs and budget. There are various options available, ranging from basic tracking tools to comprehensive affiliate marketing platforms. Consider factors such as tracking accuracy, features, integration capabilities, user-friendliness, and customer support. Popular tracking tools include Google Analytics, Voluum, ClickMeter, and AffTrack.

Install Tracking Codes: Once you've selected a tracking tool, follow the instructions provided by the tool's documentation or support team to install the tracking code on your website or landing pages. The tracking code is typically a snippet of JavaScript that collects data and sends it to the tracking tool's platform. Make sure the code is properly implemented on all relevant pages to ensure accurate tracking.

Set Up Conversion Tracking: Configure conversion tracking to monitor the performance of your affiliate campaigns. This involves setting up conversion goals or events within your tracking tool. Specify the actions you consider as conversions, such as completed purchases, form submissions, or email sign-ups. Assign unique conversion identifiers or tags to each goal for accurate tracking.

Generate Tracking Links: Generate unique tracking links for each affiliate promotion or campaign. These links typically include parameters or variables that carry information about the traffic source, campaign, and affiliate ID. This allows you to attribute conversions to specific affiliates and analyze the effectiveness of different promotional channels. Most tracking tools provide built-in link generation features or offer URL customization options.

Test and Validate Tracking: Test your tracking setup to ensure accuracy and reliability. Click on your tracking links and complete the desired actions to verify that the data is captured correctly. Monitor the data in your tracking tool's dashboard or reports to confirm that conversions are recorded accurately. Testing and validation are crucial to ensure that you can trust the data you receive for analysis and optimization.

Integrate with Affiliate Networks or Platforms: If you work with affiliate networks or platforms, set up integration with your tracking tool. This integration allows for seamless tracking of conversions, affiliate commissions, and other performance metrics. Follow the integration guidelines provided by your tracking tool and affiliate network to ensure proper data synchronization.

Customize and Analyze Reports:
Customize the reporting features of your
tracking tool to generate insightful reports
that align with your tracking goals. Create
dashboards or reports that provide a
comprehensive overview of key
performance indicators, such as clicks,
conversions, conversion rates, revenue,
and ROI. Analyze the data regularly to
identify trends, patterns, and areas for
improvement.

Optimize Based on Insights: Utilize the
data and insights obtained from your
tracking tool to optimize your affiliate
marketing strategies. Identify high-
performing campaigns, traffic sources, or
affiliate partnerships and allocate
resources accordingly. Make data-driven
decisions to refine your targeting, creative
assets, landing pages, or promotional
channels. Continuously monitor and adjust
your campaigns based on the insights
gained from tracking data.

Stay Up-to-Date: Stay informed about updates and new features in your tracking tool or software. Regularly check for software updates, attend webinars or training sessions, and join relevant communities or forums to learn from industry experts and fellow affiliate marketers. Keeping up-to-date with the latest advancements ensures that you maximize the benefits of your tracking tools.

Setting up tracking tools and software is essential for accurate measurement, analysis, and optimization in affiliate marketing. By implementing these steps, you can effectively track the performance of your campaigns, identify areas for improvement, and make informed decisions to achieve your affiliate marketing goals.

Analyzing Data to Measure Performance

Analyzing data is a critical aspect of affiliate marketing, allowing you to measure the performance of your campaigns, identify trends, and make data-driven decisions. By effectively analyzing the data you collect, you can gain valuable insights into your affiliate marketing efforts and optimize your strategies for better results. ***Here are the key steps to analyzing data to measure performance***:

Set Clear Objectives: Before diving into data analysis, establish clear objectives for what you want to achieve with your affiliate marketing campaigns. Define key performance indicators (KPIs) that align with your goals, such as click-through rates, conversion rates, sales, revenue, or return on investment (ROI).

Clear objectives provide a framework for data analysis and help you focus on relevant metrics.

Gather Relevant Data: Collect data from various sources relevant to your affiliate marketing campaigns. This includes data from your tracking tools, affiliate networks or platforms, website analytics platforms (e.g., Google Analytics), and any other platforms or tools you use to monitor your campaigns. Ensure you have access to accurate and comprehensive data for analysis.

Clean and Organize Data: Clean and organize the data you have collected to ensure its quality and usability. Remove any duplicates, errors, or irrelevant data points that may skew your analysis. Organize the data in a structured manner, labeling each data point and organizing it into relevant categories. This step sets the foundation for effective data analysis.

Define Metrics and Dimensions:
Determine the metrics and dimensions that are relevant to your analysis. Metrics are quantitative measurements of specific aspects, such as clicks, conversions, or revenue. Dimensions provide context to the metrics and include elements like traffic sources, campaign names, affiliate IDs, or customer demographics. Choose the metrics and dimensions that align with your objectives and help you gain meaningful insights.

Utilize Data Visualization: Visualize your data using charts, graphs, or dashboards to make it easier to interpret and understand. Data visualization helps identify patterns, trends, or anomalies at a glance. Use appropriate visualizations for different types of data, such as line charts for trends over time, bar charts for comparisons, or pie charts for proportional data. Visualizations provide a clearer picture of your performance metrics.

Identify Performance Trends: Analyze your data to identify performance trends over time. Look for patterns in your KPIs, such as changes in click-through rates, conversion rates, or revenue. Identify factors that may have influenced these trends, such as promotional activities, traffic sources, or campaign optimizations. Understanding performance trends helps you evaluate the effectiveness of your strategies.

Segment and Compare Data: Segment your data to gain deeper insights into specific aspects of your affiliate marketing campaigns. Compare performance metrics across different segments, such as traffic sources, affiliate partnerships, campaign types, or customer demographics. This analysis helps identify high-performing segments, as well as areas that may require optimization or adjustment.

Conduct A/B Testing: Perform A/B testing to evaluate the impact of different variations of your campaigns or strategies. Split your audience into different groups and test different elements, such as ad copy, visuals, landing page layouts, or promotional offers. Measure the performance of each variation and identify the most effective approaches. A/B testing helps optimize your campaigns based on data-driven results.

Identify Opportunities for Improvement: Based on your data analysis, identify opportunities for improvement in your affiliate marketing efforts. Identify underperforming campaigns, traffic sources, or affiliate partnerships that may need adjustments or optimizations. Look for areas where small changes can lead to significant improvements in performance. Focus on data-driven insights to guide your decision-making process.

Iterate and Optimize: Continuously iterate and optimize your affiliate marketing strategies based on your data analysis. Implement changes and adjustments to improve performance. Monitor the impact of your optimizations and assess the results through ongoing data analysis. This iterative process allows you to refine your strategies, maximize your ROI, and achieve your affiliate marketing goals.

Analyzing data to measure performance is essential for affiliate marketers to evaluate the effectiveness of their campaigns, identify areas for improvement, and optimize their strategies. By following these steps and leveraging data-driven insights, you can make informed decisions, drive better results, and achieve success in your affiliate marketing endeavors.

Making Data-Driven Decisions for Optimization

In the world of affiliate marketing, making data-driven decisions is crucial for optimizing your campaigns and achieving better results. By analyzing and interpreting the data you collect, you can gain valuable insights that guide your decision-making process. ***Here are the key steps to making data-driven decisions for optimization***:

Define Your Optimization Goals: Clearly define your optimization goals based on the desired outcomes you want to achieve. Whether it's increasing click-through rates, improving conversion rates, boosting revenue, or maximizing return on investment (ROI), having well-defined goals provides a focus for your data analysis and decision-making.

Collect Relevant Data: Gather relevant data from various sources, including your tracking tools, website analytics platforms, affiliate networks or platforms, and any other tools or platforms you use to monitor your campaigns. Ensure that the data you collect aligns with your optimization goals and covers the key metrics and dimensions you need to evaluate.

Analyze Performance Metrics: Dive into the data and analyze performance metrics that are relevant to your optimization goals. This may include click-through rates, conversion rates, revenue, average order value, traffic sources, campaign performance, and more. Identify trends, patterns, and areas of improvement within the data.

Segment and Compare Data: Segment your data based on different variables such as traffic sources, campaign types, affiliate partnerships, customer demographics, or any other relevant dimensions.

Compare the performance metrics across these segments to identify high-performing areas and areas that need optimization. This segmentation allows for more targeted and effective optimization strategies.

Identify Key Performance Drivers: Determine the key factors that contribute to the performance of your affiliate marketing campaigns. Analyze the relationships between different variables to understand what drives success. For example, identify the traffic sources that generate the most conversions or the campaign elements that lead to higher click-through rates. Understanding these drivers helps you prioritize your optimization efforts.

Conduct A/B Testing: Implement A/B testing to evaluate different variations of your campaigns or strategies. Test different elements such as ad copy, visuals, call-to-action buttons, landing page designs, or promotional offers. Measure the performance of each variation and identify the ones that yield the best results. A/B testing allows you to optimize your campaigns based on empirical evidence rather than assumptions.

Leverage Statistical Analysis: Utilize statistical analysis techniques to extract deeper insights from your data. Conduct significance tests, regression analysis, or correlation analysis to identify meaningful relationships and determine the statistical significance of your findings. Statistical analysis provides a more robust foundation for making data-driven decisions.

Monitor Competitor Performance: Keep an eye on the performance of your competitors to gain a broader perspective and identify potential areas of improvement. Analyze their strategies, creative approaches, targeting methods, and customer engagement tactics. Benchmark your performance against industry standards and competitor benchmarks to identify areas where you can improve and differentiate yourself.

Implement Iterative Optimization: Based on the insights gained from your data analysis, implement iterative optimization strategies. Make incremental changes to your campaigns, targeting, creative assets, landing pages, or promotional channels. Monitor the impact of these optimizations and assess their effectiveness through ongoing data analysis. Continuously iterate and refine your strategies to achieve better results.

Track and Evaluate Results: Track the results of your optimization efforts by monitoring the performance metrics that align with your goals. Evaluate the impact of your optimizations on key metrics such as click-through rates, conversion rates, revenue, or ROI.

Assess whether the changes you've made have positively influenced the performance of your affiliate marketing campaigns.

By making data-driven decisions for optimization, you can continually refine your affiliate marketing strategies and achieve better results. Data analysis empowers you to identify areas of improvement, understand what drives success, and implement targeted optimizations. By leveraging data insights, you can make informed decisions that maximize your campaign performance and ultimately drive success in the competitive world of affiliate marketing.

Chapter 10: Conversion Optimization

Understanding Conversion Rate Optimization (CRO)

Conversion Rate Optimization (CRO) is a crucial aspect of affiliate marketing that focuses on increasing the percentage of website visitors who take the desired action, such as making a purchase, subscribing to a newsletter, or filling out a form. It involves systematically improving various elements of your website or landing page to enhance user experience, engagement, and ultimately, conversions. *Here are the key points to understand about Conversion Rate Optimization*:

Definition of Conversion Rate: The conversion rate represents the percentage of website visitors who complete a specific desired action. It is calculated by dividing the number of conversions by the total number of website visitors and multiplying it by 100. CRO aims to increase this conversion rate by optimizing the user journey and removing any barriers to conversion.

Importance of CRO: Conversion Rate Optimization is essential because it allows you to maximize the value of your website traffic. Instead of solely focusing on driving more traffic, CRO helps you extract the most value from the existing visitors by increasing the likelihood of conversions. It is a cost-effective approach that can lead to significant improvements in your affiliate marketing results.

User-Centric Approach: CRO emphasizes the importance of understanding your website visitors and catering to their needs and preferences. By adopting a user-centric approach, you can identify pain points, optimize the user journey, and create a seamless and enjoyable experience for your audience.

This, in turn, increases the chances of conversions and enhances customer satisfaction.

Key Elements of CRO: CRO involves optimizing various elements on your website or landing page to drive conversions. These elements include but are not limited to:

Call-to-Action (CTA): Optimizing the design, placement, and wording of your CTA buttons to encourage visitors to take action.

Landing Page Design: Creating visually appealing, user-friendly, and persuasive landing pages that align with your campaign goals.

Content Optimization: Crafting compelling and persuasive content that highlights the benefits of the product or service you're promoting.

Forms and Checkout Process:
Simplifying and streamlining the form-filling or checkout process to reduce friction and abandonment rates.

Trust Factors: Incorporating trust elements such as customer reviews, testimonials, security badges, and guarantees to instill confidence in visitors.

Page Load Speed: Optimizing the performance and load speed of your website to provide a seamless browsing experience.

Mobile Optimization: Ensuring your website is fully optimized for mobile devices to accommodate the growing number of mobile users.

A/B Testing: A/B testing is a fundamental technique in CRO that involves comparing two versions of a webpage or element to determine which one performs better in terms of conversions. By testing different variations, such as different headlines, layouts, colors, or CTAs, you can gather data-driven insights and make informed decisions about the most effective elements to implement.

Data Analysis: Data analysis plays a critical role in CRO. By tracking and analyzing user behavior, engagement metrics, and conversion data, you can identify patterns, trends, and areas for improvement. Utilize tools like Google Analytics or heat mapping software to gain valuable insights into user interactions and make data-driven decisions.

Continuous Optimization: CRO is an ongoing process that requires continuous monitoring and optimization. Implement changes based on data insights, conduct regular A/B tests, and assess the impact of optimizations on your conversion rate. Continually iterate and refine your approach to achieve incremental improvements over time.

Understanding Conversion Rate Optimization is vital for affiliate marketers who want to maximize the value of their website traffic and increase conversions. By adopting a user-centric approach, optimizing key elements, conducting A/B tests, and analyzing data, you can continuously improve your website's conversion rate and drive better results in your affiliate marketing campaigns.

A/B Testing and Experimentation

A/B testing, also known as split testing, is a powerful technique in affiliate marketing that allows you to compare two or more variations of a webpage, element, or campaign to determine which one performs better in terms of conversions or other key metrics. It is an essential component of data-driven decision-making and enables you to optimize your affiliate marketing efforts. *Here's what you need to know about A/B testing and experimentation*:

A/B Testing Basics: A/B testing involves creating multiple variations of a webpage, ad, email, or any other marketing element and randomly splitting your audience into different groups. Each group is shown a different version, and their responses are measured and compared to identify the most effective variation. Typically, the original version (control) is compared against one or more variations (variants) to determine which one yields better results.

Testing Elements: A/B testing allows you to test various elements to understand their impact on conversion rates or other desired outcomes. Common elements to test include headlines, images, calls-to-action, layouts, colors, form fields, pricing, and promotional offers. By systematically testing these elements, you can identify the optimal configuration that resonates with your audience and drives higher conversions.

Hypothesis Development: A successful A/B test starts with a clear hypothesis. Formulate a hypothesis that outlines the expected impact of the changes you plan to test. For example, if you believe that a different headline will capture more attention and drive higher click-through rates, state that in your hypothesis.

A well-defined hypothesis helps you focus your testing efforts and guides your analysis of the results.

Sample Size and Statistical Significance: To ensure reliable results, it's important to have an adequate sample size for your A/B test. The sample size should be large enough to detect meaningful differences and achieve statistical significance. Statistical significance determines whether the observed differences in conversion rates between variations are statistically significant or simply due to chance. Use online calculators or statistical tools to determine the required sample size for your tests.

Test Duration: The duration of your A/B test should be long enough to capture a representative sample of your audience and account for any potential day-to-day variations. Avoid prematurely ending tests before reaching statistical significance, as it may lead to inconclusive or inaccurate results. Consider factors such as your website traffic, conversion rates, and desired confidence level when determining the appropriate test duration.

Analyzing Results: Once your A/B test is complete, analyze the results to draw meaningful insights. Compare the performance metrics of the control and variant(s) and identify any statistically significant differences. Pay attention to conversion rates, click-through rates, bounce rates, engagement metrics, or any other relevant metrics based on your objectives. Data analysis tools and statistical techniques can help interpret the results accurately.

Implementing Winners: If a variant outperforms the control and shows statistically significant improvements, consider implementing the winning variation as the default. Apply the successful changes to your affiliate marketing campaigns, website, or other marketing channels. Continuously monitor the performance of the implemented changes and iterate further if necessary.

Iterative Testing: A/B testing is an iterative process that allows you to continually optimize your affiliate marketing strategies. Once you implement a winning variation, you can further test other elements or variations to refine your approach. Constantly seek new opportunities for improvement and employ A/B testing as a regular practice to drive continuous enhancements and better results.

A/B testing and experimentation empower affiliate marketers to make data-driven decisions and optimize their campaigns for improved performance. By testing different variations, analyzing results, and implementing the winning variations, you can refine your strategies, increase conversions, and ultimately maximize the success of your affiliate marketing efforts.

Improving Landing Page and Website Conversions

Landing pages and websites play a crucial role in affiliate marketing as they serve as the gateway for converting visitors into customers or leads. Optimizing these digital assets can significantly improve conversion rates and boost the effectiveness of your affiliate marketing efforts. ***Here are some key strategies to consider for improving landing page and website conversions***:

Clear and Compelling Messaging: Craft clear and compelling messaging that clearly communicates the value proposition of your affiliate offer. Use concise and persuasive language to highlight the benefits, features, and unique selling points. Make it easy for visitors to understand what they can gain by taking the desired action on your landing page or website.

Attention-Grabbing Headlines: Create attention-grabbing headlines that immediately capture the interest of visitors. Your headline should be compelling and directly related to the affiliate offer. It should evoke curiosity, address a pain point, or promise a solution. Experiment with different headlines through A/B testing to identify the most effective ones.

Engaging Visuals: Utilize high-quality and relevant visuals, such as images, videos, or infographics, to enhance the visual appeal of your landing page or website. Visuals should complement the messaging and help convey the value proposition. Use captivating images that resonate with your target audience and support the conversion goal.

Clear Call-to-Action (CTA): Place a clear and prominent call-to-action (CTA) on your landing page or website.

The CTA should stand out visually and use action-oriented language that compels visitors to take the desired action. Make sure the CTA button is easily clickable and that its purpose is clearly defined. Experiment with different CTA designs, wording, and placement to optimize conversions.

Streamlined Conversion Process: Simplify the conversion process by reducing the number of form fields or steps required to complete the desired action. Minimize friction and remove any unnecessary barriers that may deter visitors from converting. Optimize the user experience to make it effortless and intuitive for users to complete the conversion process.

Social Proof and Testimonials: Incorporate social proof elements such as customer testimonials, reviews, ratings, or case studies to build trust and credibility.

Positive feedback from satisfied customers can reassure potential customers and increase their confidence in your affiliate offer. Display testimonials prominently on your landing page or website to boost conversions.

Mobile Optimization: With the increasing use of mobile devices, it is crucial to ensure that your landing pages and websites are fully optimized for mobile users. Implement responsive design techniques to ensure a seamless and user-friendly experience across different screen sizes. Mobile-friendly pages improve user engagement and reduce bounce rates, leading to higher conversions.

Page Load Speed: Optimize the loading speed of your landing pages and website to prevent visitors from leaving due to slow loading times. Minimize file sizes, leverage caching mechanisms, and optimize code to improve page load speed.

Faster-loading pages not only improve the user experience but also contribute to better search engine rankings.

Trust and Security: Build trust with your visitors by prominently displaying trust signals such as security badges, privacy policies, or encryption symbols. Assure users that their personal information is safe and secure when interacting with your landing page or website. Clear privacy policies and transparent data handling practices can increase visitor confidence and encourage conversions.

Data-Driven Optimization: Continuously monitor and analyze the performance of your landing pages and website using analytics tools. Track key metrics such as conversion rates, bounce rates, average time on page, and click-through rates to gain insights into user behavior. Identify areas of improvement and conduct A/B tests to experiment with different elements and optimize for higher conversions.

By implementing these strategies, you can enhance the effectiveness of your landing pages and website, leading to improved conversion rates and increased success in your affiliate marketing endeavors. Regularly test, analyze, and optimize your digital assets to maximize their impact on driving conversions and achieving your affiliate marketing goals.

Establishing Yourself as an Authority in Your Niche

In the competitive world of affiliate marketing, establishing yourself as an authority in your niche can significantly enhance your credibility, attract a loyal audience, and ultimately drive more conversions. Becoming an authority demonstrates your expertise, builds trust with your audience, and sets you apart from competitors. ***Here are some strategies to establish yourself as an authority in your niche***:

In-Depth Knowledge: Develop a deep understanding of your niche by conducting thorough research, staying up-to-date with industry trends, and immersing yourself in relevant topics. Become a reliable source of information by continuously expanding your knowledge and expertise.

Share valuable insights, tips, and strategies that showcase your understanding of the niche.

High-Quality Content Creation: Consistently produce high-quality content that educates, informs, and engages your audience. Create content in various formats, such as blog posts, videos, podcasts, or infographics, catering to different preferences. Offer unique perspectives, original ideas, and valuable solutions to the challenges faced by your target audience. Your content should be well-researched, well-written, and visually appealing.

Thought Leadership: Position yourself as a thought leader by sharing your opinions, insights, and predictions about your niche. Express your unique viewpoint and provide valuable commentary on industry developments. Write thought-provoking articles, participate in relevant discussions, and contribute to industry forums or social media groups. Engage with your audience and establish yourself as a trusted voice in your niche.

Guest Blogging and Collaborations: Seek opportunities to guest blog on influential websites or collaborate with other experts in your niche. Guest blogging allows you to reach a wider audience and gain exposure to new potential followers. Collaborating with other experts not only enhances your credibility but also provides valuable networking opportunities. Share your expertise, contribute to industry publications, and engage with other thought leaders.

Consistent Branding: Develop a strong personal brand that reflects your expertise and establishes trust with your audience. Maintain consistent branding across your website, social media profiles, and content. Use professional branding elements such as a logo, color scheme, and a cohesive visual identity. Consistent branding helps create a recognizable and memorable presence in your niche.

Engage with Your Audience: Actively engage with your audience through comments, social media interactions, and email communication. Respond to questions, provide helpful insights, and foster meaningful conversations. Act as a resource and build relationships with your followers. Engaging with your audience demonstrates your commitment to helping them and reinforces your authority status.

Social Proof: Leverage social proof to enhance your authority status. Share testimonials, success stories, case studies, or user-generated content that demonstrates the positive impact of your expertise. Encourage satisfied customers or followers to provide testimonials or reviews that highlight the value you provide.

Social proof validates your authority and builds trust with potential customers.

Speaking Engagements and Webinars: Seek opportunities to speak at industry conferences, webinars, or podcasts. Sharing your knowledge and expertise through speaking engagements allows you to reach a wider audience and establish yourself as an authority figure. Deliver insightful presentations, share valuable strategies, and engage with the audience to build credibility and visibility.

Continuous Learning and Growth: Stay committed to continuous learning and personal growth within your niche. Attend industry events, participate in training programs, and pursue certifications or advanced education. Stay ahead of the curve by being aware of emerging trends and advancements in your field. Your dedication to ongoing learning reinforces your authority and keeps you at the forefront of your niche.

Networking and Collaboration: Network with other professionals, influencers, and experts in your niche. Attend industry events, join relevant communities, and establish meaningful connections. Collaborate on projects, co-create content, or host joint webinars with others in your field. Building relationships and collaborating with like-minded individuals strengthens your authority and expands your reach.

By implementing these strategies, you can establish yourself as a respected authority in your niche. Through continuous learning, high-quality content creation, thought leadership, and engagement with your audience, you will build trust, attract a loyal following, and drive more conversions in your affiliate marketing endeavors.

Building Trust with Your Audience

Trust is a crucial element in affiliate marketing as it establishes credibility, fosters long-term relationships, and encourages conversions. When your audience trusts you, they are more likely to engage with your recommendations and make purchasing decisions based on your suggestions. *Here are some effective strategies for building trust with your audience*:

Consistent and Transparent Communication: Establish consistent communication with your audience across various channels, including your website, social media platforms, and email marketing. Be transparent about your affiliate partnerships and disclose any potential conflicts of interest. Share valuable and unbiased information, providing your audience with genuine insights and recommendations.

Authenticity and Integrity: Be authentic in your interactions and content creation. Share personal stories, experiences, and challenges that demonstrate your authenticity. Avoid promoting products or services solely for monetary gain. Prioritize integrity by recommending only products or services that you genuinely believe in and that align with your audience's needs and interests.

Quality Content: Create high-quality, valuable content that addresses your audience's pain points, educates them, and offers solutions to their problems. Ensure that your content is well-researched, accurate, and up-to-date. By consistently delivering valuable information, you establish yourself as a reliable source of expertise in your niche.

Social Proof: Utilize social proof to showcase the positive experiences of your satisfied customers or clients.

Share testimonials, reviews, case studies, or success stories that highlight the effectiveness and value of the products or services you promote. Social proof acts as evidence that others have benefited from your recommendations, enhancing trust among your audience.

Engage and Respond: Actively engage with your audience by responding to comments, messages, and inquiries promptly. Show genuine interest in their questions and concerns. Encourage open dialogue, foster discussions, and provide helpful and informative responses. Engaging with your audience demonstrates your accessibility and willingness to assist them.

Authentic Testimonials and Reviews: Display authentic testimonials and reviews from real customers or clients who have used the products or services you promote. Ensure that these testimonials are genuine and transparent, as fake or misleading testimonials can severely damage trust. Authentic testimonials provide social proof and validate the quality and effectiveness of the products or services.

Privacy and Data Security: Prioritize the privacy and data security of your audience. Clearly communicate your data handling practices, assure users that their information is secure, and comply with relevant data protection regulations. Implement security measures such as SSL certificates on your website to instill confidence in your audience that their personal information is safeguarded.

Expertise and Authority: Demonstrate your expertise and authority in your niche by consistently sharing valuable insights, research, and industry updates. Provide accurate and reliable information that helps your audience make informed decisions. Position yourself as a knowledgeable resource and thought leader within your field.

Consistency and Reliability: Be consistent in your messaging, content delivery, and overall brand presence. Consistency builds familiarity and trust among your audience. Deliver on your promises, meet expectations, and ensure that the products or services you recommend align with the quality you promote. Reliable recommendations reinforce trust in your audience's eyes.

Honesty About Limitations: Be honest about the limitations of the products or services you promote. If there are any drawbacks or downsides, acknowledge them openly. Being transparent about limitations shows that you prioritize your audience's best interests over solely promoting affiliate offers.

Building trust with your audience takes time and effort. By consistently providing valuable content, engaging authentically, showcasing social proof, and prioritizing transparency and integrity, you can establish a strong foundation of trust that fosters long-term relationships and boosts conversions in your affiliate marketing journey.

Leveraging Social Proof and Testimonials

Social proof and testimonials are powerful tools in affiliate marketing that can significantly influence the purchasing decisions of your audience.

They provide evidence that others have had positive experiences with the products or services you promote, building trust and credibility. ***Here are some effective ways to leverage social proof and testimonials in your affiliate marketing efforts***:

Genuine Testimonials: Collect genuine testimonials from satisfied customers or clients who have used the products or services you promote. Reach out to your audience and request feedback or testimonials based on their experiences. Authentic testimonials add credibility to your recommendations and demonstrate the value others have derived from the products or services.

Display Testimonials Strategically: Place testimonials strategically on your website, landing pages, or product review pages. Consider using testimonial snippets or quotes alongside relevant product features or benefits. Highlight the most compelling and relevant testimonials to capture the attention of your audience. Visual elements such as photos or videos can further enhance the authenticity and impact of the testimonials.

Case Studies and Success Stories: Share detailed case studies or success stories that showcase how individuals or businesses have achieved positive results through the products or services you promote. Provide specific details about the challenges faced, the solutions implemented, and the measurable outcomes. Case studies offer in-depth insights into the effectiveness and benefits of the products or services.

Influencer Endorsements: Collaborate with influencers or industry experts who have a strong following and reputation in your niche. Seek endorsements or product reviews from these influencers to tap into their established credibility and reach. Influencer endorsements can significantly boost trust and generate interest in the products or services you promote.

User-Generated Content: Encourage your audience to share their experiences with the products or services by creating user-generated content campaigns. Ask them to post reviews, testimonials, or social media posts with specific hashtags or tags. User-generated content adds an authentic and relatable touch, as it comes directly from real users.

Video Testimonials: Video testimonials can have a profound impact on your audience. Record video testimonials of satisfied customers or clients discussing their positive experiences with the products or services. Video testimonials add a personal touch, allowing your audience to see and hear real people sharing their genuine feedback. This form of social proof can be highly persuasive and engaging.

Social Media Mentions and Reviews:
Monitor social media platforms for
mentions, tags, or reviews related to the
products or services you promote. Share
positive reviews or testimonials on your
social media profiles to highlight the
satisfaction of your customers. Encourage
your audience to leave reviews or ratings
on platforms such as Facebook, Google, or
industry-specific review sites.

Ratings and Reviews Integration:
Incorporate rating and review systems on
your website or product pages to allow
customers to provide feedback and ratings.
Highlight the average rating or positive
reviews prominently. Integrating rating
and review systems not only provides
social proof but also encourages user
engagement and interaction.

Case Study Partnerships: Collaborate
with the product or service providers to
create case studies or success stories
together.

This mutually beneficial partnership allows you to showcase real-world examples of successful implementations while strengthening your relationship with the product or service provider. It also provides valuable content that can attract and persuade your audience.

Testimonial Videos from Industry Experts: Seek testimonials or endorsements from industry experts who have established credibility and expertise in your niche. Their recommendations carry weight and influence among your audience. Request video testimonials from these experts, where they share their positive experiences and endorse the products or services.

When leveraging social proof and testimonials, always prioritize authenticity and transparency. Ensure that the testimonials are genuine, and the experiences shared align with the claims you make about the products or services. Social proof and testimonials act as powerful influencers, building trust and confidence in your audience and increasing the likelihood of conversions in your affiliate marketing endeavors.

Exploring Popular Affiliate Networks

Affiliate networks play a vital role in connecting affiliate marketers with a wide range of products and services to promote. These networks act as intermediaries, facilitating partnerships between affiliates and advertisers. ***Here are some popular affiliate networks worth exploring in your affiliate marketing journey***:

Amazon Associates: As one of the largest and most well-known affiliate networks, Amazon Associates offers a vast selection of products across various categories. With its global reach and extensive product inventory, affiliates can earn commissions by promoting products available on Amazon's platform.

ShareASale: ShareASale is a popular affiliate network that hosts a diverse range of merchants across multiple industries. Affiliates can choose from thousands of affiliate programs and gain access to comprehensive reporting tools, real-time tracking, and reliable payment systems.

CJ Affiliate (formerly Commission Junction): CJ Affiliate is a widely recognized affiliate network that connects affiliates with top brands and advertisers. It offers a wide array of products and services across different niches. CJ Affiliate provides advanced reporting, tracking capabilities, and performance-based commissions.

ClickBank: ClickBank is a leading affiliate network specializing in digital products such as e-books, online courses, software, and memberships. Affiliates can browse through an extensive marketplace of products and earn commissions by promoting these digital offerings.

Rakuten Affiliate Network: Rakuten Affiliate Network (formerly LinkShare) is a global affiliate network that provides access to a wide range of merchants and brands. Affiliates can choose from various industries and verticals to find products that align with their niche. Rakuten offers robust reporting tools and a user-friendly interface.

Impact: Impact is an affiliate marketing platform that connects affiliates with brands seeking partnerships. It offers a suite of performance marketing solutions, including affiliate management, tracking, reporting, and payment automation. Impact hosts well-known brands across multiple sectors.

Awin: Awin is a prominent affiliate network that brings together affiliates and advertisers from around the world. With a vast network of merchants, Awin offers opportunities to promote a diverse range of products and services. It provides advanced tracking and reporting features, as well as a user-friendly interface.

FlexOffers: FlexOffers is an affiliate network that offers a wide range of affiliate programs in various verticals, including finance, health, fashion, and technology. Affiliates can access a large database of advertisers and enjoy features such as real-time reporting and monthly payouts.

eBay Partner Network: eBay Partner Network allows affiliates to earn commissions by promoting products listed on eBay. Affiliates can leverage eBay's extensive product inventory and benefit from the global reach of the platform. The network provides access to reporting tools, promotional materials, and performance metrics.

MaxBounty: MaxBounty is a performance-based affiliate network that specializes in cost-per-action (CPA) affiliate marketing. It offers a range of high-converting CPA offers across various niches, including lead generation, mobile apps, and trial offers. MaxBounty provides detailed reporting and weekly payments.

When exploring affiliate networks, consider factors such as the variety of products or services available, commission rates, payment methods, reporting capabilities, and the reputation and reliability of the network. It's important to read and understand the terms and conditions of each network before joining to ensure they align with your affiliate marketing goals and strategies.

By joining popular affiliate networks, you can access a wide range of affiliate programs, gain exposure to diverse product offerings, and leverage the tools and resources provided by these networks to enhance your affiliate marketing efforts.

Using Affiliate Marketing Tools and Plugins

In the world of affiliate marketing, various tools and plugins can greatly enhance your productivity, optimize your promotional efforts, and streamline your affiliate business. These tools offer features such as link management, analytics, content creation, and automation. *Here are some commonly used affiliate marketing tools and plugins that can help you succeed*:

Affiliate Link Management Tools: Link management tools such as ThirstyAffiliates, Pretty Links, and Geniuslink allow you to easily organize and track your affiliate links. These tools provide link cloaking, redirection, and analytics, ensuring that your links are professional, trackable, and optimized for better conversions.

Affiliate Networks: As mentioned earlier, affiliate networks like Amazon Associates, ShareASale, and CJ Affiliate provide comprehensive platforms for finding and managing affiliate programs. They offer reporting tools, tracking capabilities, and payment systems, simplifying your affiliate marketing operations.

Google Analytics: Google Analytics is a powerful analytics tool that allows you to track and analyze website traffic, visitor behavior, and conversion rates.

By integrating Google Analytics into your website, you can gain valuable insights into the performance of your affiliate campaigns, identify trends, and make data-driven decisions to optimize your marketing strategies.

SEO Tools: SEO tools like SEMrush, Moz, and Ahrefs can help you improve your website's visibility in search engine results. These tools provide keyword research, backlink analysis, site auditing, and competitor analysis features, enabling you to optimize your content and increase organic traffic to your affiliate site.

Content Creation Tools: Content creation tools such as Canva, Grammarly, and Hemingway Editor assist you in creating visually appealing and error-free content. Canva allows you to design professional-looking graphics and social media posts, while Grammarly and Hemingway Editor help you ensure that your written content is free from grammatical errors and is easily readable.

Email Marketing Tools: Email marketing tools like Mailchimp, ConvertKit, and AWeber enable you to build and manage your email list, create automated email sequences, and track the performance of your email campaigns. These tools provide templates, segmentation options, and analytics to help you effectively engage with your audience and promote affiliate offers.

Social Media Management Tools: Social media management tools such as Hootsuite, Buffer, and Sprout Social allow you to schedule and automate your social media posts across multiple platforms. These tools provide analytics, content curation features, and social listening capabilities, helping you maintain an active social media presence and engage with your audience effectively.

WordPress Plugins: If your affiliate site is built on WordPress, various plugins can enhance its functionality. Plugins like Yoast SEO, Rank Math, and All in One SEO Pack optimize your content for search engines and improve your site's SEO. Additionally, plugins like MonsterInsights and Google Analytics Dashboard for WP integrate Google Analytics into your WordPress dashboard for easy access to analytics data.

Heatmap and User Behavior Tools: Heatmap and user behavior tools like Hotjar and Crazy Egg provide insights into how users interact with your website. These tools create visual representations of user behavior, showing where visitors click, scroll, or spend the most time on your site. Understanding user behavior can help you optimize your site's layout and improve conversion rates.

Affiliate Management Plugins: If you plan to create and manage your own affiliate program, affiliate management plugins like AffiliateWP and Refersion can simplify the process. These plugins allow you to set up affiliate programs, track referrals, manage commissions, and provide affiliates with access to promotional materials.

When selecting affiliate marketing tools and plugins, consider your specific needs, budget, and the compatibility of the tools with your existing systems. It's important to research and read reviews to ensure that the tools you choose are reputable, reliable, and offer the features that will support your affiliate marketing goals. By leveraging these tools and plugins, you can optimize your workflow, track performance, and ultimately increase your chances of success as an affiliate marketer.

Maximizing Your Earnings Through Partnerships

In affiliate marketing, partnerships play a crucial role in expanding your reach, increasing your earning potential, and establishing yourself as a trusted authority in your niche. By forming strategic partnerships with other affiliates, influencers, and industry experts, you can leverage their audience, expertise, and resources to maximize your earnings.
Here are some key strategies to consider for maximizing your earnings through partnerships:

Collaborate with Complementary Affiliates: Identify affiliates who operate in complementary niches or target similar audiences. By collaborating with them, you can cross-promote each other's products or services, expanding your reach and tapping into new customer segments.

For example, if you're promoting fitness equipment, you could partner with an affiliate who focuses on nutrition or workout apparel.

Engage with Influencers: Influencers have a strong following and can significantly impact purchasing decisions. Partnering with relevant influencers in your niche can expose your affiliate offers to their audience, generating more leads and conversions. Reach out to influencers through personalized pitches or influencer marketing platforms, and negotiate mutually beneficial partnerships, such as sponsored content or affiliate collaborations.

Seek Joint Ventures: Consider forming joint ventures with other affiliate marketers or product creators. A joint venture involves combining resources, skills, and audiences to create a new product or launch a marketing campaign. By pooling your expertise and networks, you can generate higher profits and reach a larger audience than you would individually.

Engage in Affiliate Product Launches: Participate in affiliate product launches where multiple affiliates promote a new product or service simultaneously. These launches often offer higher commission rates, special bonuses, and dedicated promotional support. By aligning yourself with successful product launches and leveraging the buzz surrounding them, you can increase your earnings and gain exposure to a larger customer base.

Offer Value to Industry Experts: Building relationships with industry experts can open doors to new opportunities and collaborations. Provide value to experts by offering them guest posts, interviews, or testimonials for their websites or products. This can lead to reciprocal promotion, joint ventures, or endorsements from respected figures in your niche, ultimately boosting your credibility and earning potential.

Attend Affiliate Marketing Events and Conferences: Networking events and conferences focused on affiliate marketing provide valuable opportunities to meet industry professionals, potential partners, and affiliate program managers. Engage in conversations, exchange contact information, and explore potential collaboration opportunities. Building personal connections and nurturing relationships can lead to fruitful partnerships that maximize your earnings.

Negotiate Higher Commission Rates: As you establish yourself as a successful affiliate marketer, you can negotiate higher commission rates with advertisers or affiliate programs. Showcase your performance metrics, conversion rates, and the value you bring to their brand.

Higher commission rates directly impact your earnings, so don't hesitate to advocate for fair compensation based on your results.

Provide Exclusive Bonuses and Incentives: Offer exclusive bonuses or incentives to potential customers who purchase through your affiliate links. These can be in the form of e-books, video courses, or additional products or services that complement the affiliate offer. Exclusive bonuses add value to the customer's purchase, incentivizing them to choose your affiliate link over others.

Continuously Nurture Partnerships: Building successful partnerships is an ongoing process. Continuously nurture your relationships with partners by offering support, sharing insights, and collaborating on new projects. Regular communication and mutual support foster long-term partnerships that can lead to increased earnings and shared success.

Remember, successful partnerships are built on trust, mutual benefit, and clear communication. Be selective when choosing partners, ensuring that their values align with yours and that they have a genuine interest in supporting your success. By maximizing your earnings through partnerships, you can tap into new audiences, enhance your credibility, and create a network of collaborators who can contribute to your long-term affiliate marketing success.

Understanding Affiliate Marketing Regulations

In the world of affiliate marketing, it's important to have a clear understanding of the regulations and guidelines that govern the industry. Adhering to these regulations not only ensures ethical business practices but also protects your reputation and minimizes the risk of legal issues. *Here are some key aspects of affiliate marketing regulations to be aware of*:

Federal Trade Commission (FTC) Guidelines: The FTC is a regulatory agency in the United States that enforces laws related to advertising, marketing, and consumer protection. The FTC requires affiliates to disclose their relationship with advertisers and provide transparent and honest information to consumers.

This means clearly disclosing that you may earn a commission from affiliate links and ensuring that your promotional content is truthful and not misleading.

Disclosure Requirements: Affiliate marketers must clearly and conspicuously disclose their affiliate relationships to consumers. Disclosures should be placed in a prominent location where consumers can easily notice them, such as within blog posts, social media posts, or email newsletters. Disclosures should be clear, concise, and easy to understand, using language that the average consumer can comprehend.

Endorsement Guidelines: When promoting products or services as an affiliate, it's essential to follow endorsement guidelines. Endorsements should accurately reflect your personal experience and opinions. If you haven't personally used the product or service, you should clearly disclose this fact to avoid misleading consumers. Additionally, if you receive free products or compensation in exchange for a review or endorsement, you must disclose this relationship to maintain transparency.

Data Protection and Privacy Laws: Affiliate marketers often collect and process consumer data, such as email addresses or cookies. It's crucial to comply with applicable data protection and privacy laws, such as the General Data Protection Regulation (GDPR) in the European Union. Obtain explicit consent when collecting personal data, provide clear privacy policies, and handle consumer data responsibly and securely.

Compliance with Advertising Laws: Affiliate marketers should also comply with general advertising laws, such as those related to false or deceptive advertising, trademark infringement, or copyright violations. Avoid making false claims, using misleading graphics, or infringing upon intellectual property rights. Ensure that your marketing practices are lawful, ethical, and respect the rights of others.

Affiliate Program Terms and Conditions: Each affiliate program may have its own terms and conditions that affiliates must adhere to. These terms often include guidelines on how to promote the products or services, restrictions on certain advertising methods, and the use of trademarks or copyrighted materials. Read and understand the terms and conditions of each affiliate program you join to ensure compliance.

Stay Informed and Seek Legal Advice: Affiliate marketing regulations may vary by country, region, or platform. Stay updated on relevant laws and guidelines, as they can change over time. Consult legal professionals or industry experts if you have specific questions or concerns about compliance in your jurisdiction.

By understanding and adhering to affiliate marketing regulations, you can build a reputable and trustworthy affiliate business. Complying with regulations not only protects you from legal repercussions but also fosters transparency, builds consumer trust, and promotes a sustainable affiliate marketing ecosystem. Remember, maintaining ethical practices is essential for long-term success in the affiliate marketing industry.

Disclosing Affiliate Relationships and Disclaimers

Transparency is a fundamental principle in affiliate marketing, and one of the key aspects of maintaining transparency is disclosing your affiliate relationships to your audience. Clear and honest disclosure ensures that consumers understand the nature of your relationship with the products or services you promote and helps build trust. ***Here's a guide to disclosing affiliate relationships and using disclaimers effectively***:

Clearly State Affiliate Relationships: It's crucial to explicitly disclose that you may earn a commission or receive compensation when someone makes a purchase through your affiliate links. This disclosure should be prominent and easy for your audience to notice. ***You can include it in various formats, such as***:

Disclosure statements within blog posts or articles.

Clear language in social media captions or bios.

Disclaimer banners or pop-ups on your website.

Disclosures in email newsletters or promotional content.

Use Clear and Concise Language: The language you use in your disclosures should be straightforward and easily understandable by the average consumer. Avoid technical jargon or ambiguous phrases. Clearly state that you may receive a commission or compensation when someone clicks on your affiliate links and makes a purchase.

Place Disclosures in Prominent Locations: Ensure that your disclosures are placed in prominent and easily noticeable locations. For blog posts or articles, consider placing the disclosure at the beginning of the content or before the first affiliate link. In social media posts, place the disclosure near the affiliate link or at the beginning of the caption. The goal is to make it clear to your audience before they engage with your content.

Use Visual Cues or Labels: Enhance the visibility of your disclosures by using visual cues or labels. For example, you can use a "Disclosure" or "Affiliate" label at the beginning of your content or next to the affiliate links. This helps draw attention to the disclosure and signals to your audience that there is an affiliate relationship involved.

Be Transparent About Product Reviews: If you provide product reviews or endorsements, make it clear whether you have personally used the product or if it's based on other forms of research. Disclose any relationships with the product manufacturer or advertiser that could influence your review. Transparency in product reviews is essential to maintain credibility and trust with your audience.

Follow Platform-Specific Guidelines: Different platforms, such as social media networks, may have specific guidelines regarding affiliate disclosure. Familiarize yourself with these guidelines and ensure compliance. For example, on platforms like Instagram or YouTube, you may need to use specific hashtags like #ad or #affiliate to disclose your relationships.

Update and Review Disclosures Regularly: As your affiliate marketing activities evolve or new partnerships are formed, make sure to update and review your disclosures regularly. Stay up-to-date with changes in regulations or platform requirements to ensure your disclosure practices remain compliant and effective.

Remember, the primary goal of disclosing affiliate relationships is to provide transparency and maintain trust with your audience. By being open and honest about your affiliations, you demonstrate your commitment to ethical marketing practices and help your audience make informed decisions. Effective disclosure practices not only protect your reputation but also contribute to the long-term success of your affiliate marketing endeavors.

Ensuring Compliance with FTC Guidelines

Complying with the Federal Trade Commission (FTC) guidelines is crucial for maintaining ethical and legal practices in affiliate marketing. The FTC is responsible for regulating advertising, marketing, and consumer protection in the United States.

Here are some key steps to ensure compliance with FTC guidelines:

Understand FTC Disclosure Requirements: Familiarize yourself with the FTC's guidelines on disclosure. The FTC requires clear and conspicuous disclosure of your affiliate relationships to consumers. Disclosures should be placed in a location where they are easily noticeable and understandable, such as within blog posts, social media posts, or email newsletters.

The language used should be clear, concise, and readily comprehensible to the average consumer.

Disclose Affiliate Relationships Clearly: Clearly disclose that you may earn a commission or receive compensation when someone makes a purchase through your affiliate links. Avoid vague or ambiguous language that may confuse or mislead consumers.
Use terms like "affiliate," "partner," or "commission" to clearly indicate the nature of the relationship.

Prominently Display Disclosures: Place your disclosures in a prominent location where they are highly visible and easily noticed by your audience. In blog posts, consider placing the disclosure at the beginning of the content or before the first affiliate link. On social media platforms, position the disclosure near the affiliate link or at the beginning of the caption.

The goal is to ensure consumers see the disclosure before engaging with your content.

Use Visual Cues or Labels: Enhance the visibility of your disclosures by using visual cues or labels that clearly indicate the presence of an affiliate relationship. Consider using labels like "Disclosure," "Affiliate," or icons that symbolize compensation.
Visual cues draw attention to the disclosure and help consumers recognize its significance.

Disclose Free Products or Compensation: If you receive free products or compensation in exchange for a review or endorsement, disclose this relationship to your audience. Clearly state any material connections or incentives that may influence your promotion of a product or service.

Transparency regarding the benefits you receive helps consumers evaluate the objectivity of your recommendations.

Regularly Review and Update Disclosures: Review your disclosure practices regularly to ensure ongoing compliance with FTC guidelines. As your affiliate partnerships change or new regulations are introduced, make necessary updates to your disclosures. Stay informed about changes in FTC requirements and best practices to ensure your disclosure practices remain accurate and up to date.

Educate Yourself and Seek Legal Advice: Stay informed about FTC guidelines and seek legal advice if you have specific questions or concerns about compliance. The FTC website provides resources and guidance on advertising and marketing practices.

Consulting legal professionals who specialize in advertising or digital marketing can provide further insights and help ensure your compliance.

Remember, compliance with FTC guidelines is essential for maintaining trust with your audience and protecting your business from legal repercussions. By disclosing your affiliate relationships transparently and adhering to FTC requirements, you demonstrate your commitment to ethical marketing practices and build a solid foundation for long-term success in affiliate marketing.

Strategies for Scaling Your Affiliate Business

Scaling your affiliate business involves expanding your reach, increasing your earnings, and achieving long-term growth. While success in affiliate marketing requires time and effort, implementing effective scaling strategies can help accelerate your progress. ***Here are some strategies to consider when scaling your affiliate business***:

Diversify Your Affiliate Programs: Instead of relying on a single affiliate program, explore multiple programs within your niche. This allows you to diversify your income streams and leverage different products or services. Look for programs that align with your audience's interests and offer competitive commission rates.

Expand Your Content Creation:
Increase the quantity and quality of your content to attract a wider audience and establish yourself as an authority in your niche. Create a content strategy that incorporates various formats such as blog posts, videos, podcasts, and social media content. Consistently publish valuable and engaging content that resonates with your target audience.

Build an Email List: Focus on building an email list of engaged subscribers who are interested in your niche. Offer valuable incentives, such as exclusive content, discounts, or free resources, to encourage visitors to sign up. Nurture your email list by providing regular updates, relevant content, and personalized recommendations that align with their interests.

Invest in Paid Advertising: Consider allocating a portion of your budget towards paid advertising to reach a broader audience. Platforms like Google Ads, social media ads, or native advertising networks can help drive targeted traffic to your affiliate offers. Monitor and optimize your campaigns to ensure a positive return on investment (ROI).

Collaborate with Influencers: Partner with influencers or bloggers within your niche to expand your reach and tap into their existing audience. Collaborate on joint content, guest posting, or affiliate promotions. Influencer partnerships can help generate more exposure, increase credibility, and attract new customers to your affiliate offers.

Explore New Traffic Generation Methods: Continuously explore and experiment with different traffic generation methods to diversify your traffic sources. This may include search engine optimization (SEO), social media marketing, content syndication, guest blogging, podcast appearances, or leveraging emerging platforms and trends. Be open to testing new channels and tactics to discover what works best for your business.

Optimize Conversion Rates: Focus on optimizing your conversion rates by analyzing and improving your sales funnels, landing pages, and call-to-action strategies. Test different elements, such as headlines, visuals, copywriting, and placement of affiliate links, to improve conversions. Implement A/B testing and track key metrics to identify areas for improvement.

Automate and Outsource Tasks: As your business grows, consider automating repetitive tasks and outsourcing certain activities to free up your time for higher-value tasks. Utilize automation tools for email marketing, social media scheduling, analytics, and reporting. Delegate tasks like content creation, graphic design, or technical aspects to freelancers or virtual assistants.

Monitor Analytics and KPIs: Regularly analyze your performance metrics, such as click-through rates, conversion rates, average order value, and earnings per click. Use analytics tools and affiliate network reports to gain insights into what is working well and what needs improvement. Make data-driven decisions based on your findings to optimize your strategies and maximize your earnings.

Stay Updated and Learn Continuously: Affiliate marketing is a dynamic and evolving industry. Stay updated with industry trends, algorithm changes, and new marketing techniques. Attend conferences, webinars, and online courses to expand your knowledge and stay ahead of the curve. Continuous learning and adapting to new strategies will position you for ongoing growth.

Scaling your affiliate business requires a combination of strategic planning, consistent effort, and continuous optimization. By diversifying your income streams, expanding your reach, and focusing on conversion optimization, you can build a scalable affiliate business that generates sustainable revenue and long-term success.

Outsourcing Tasks and Building a Team

As your affiliate marketing business grows, you may reach a point where outsourcing tasks and building a team becomes necessary to scale effectively. Outsourcing and delegating certain responsibilities allow you to focus on high-value activities and leverage the expertise of others. *Here are some key considerations when it comes to outsourcing tasks and building a team*:

Identify Tasks for Outsourcing: Start by identifying tasks that are time-consuming or outside your area of expertise. Common tasks that can be outsourced include content creation, graphic design, website development, social media management, customer support, and administrative tasks. Determine which tasks are best suited for outsourcing based on your skills, time availability, and budget.

Determine Budget and Resources:
Assess your budget and resources to
determine how much you can allocate
towards outsourcing. Consider the long-
term benefits of outsourcing in terms of
time saved and improved efficiency.
Decide whether you will hire freelancers
on a project basis or hire permanent
employees. Research the costs associated
with outsourcing and create a budget that
aligns with your business goals.

**Find Qualified Freelancers or
Employees**: Seek out freelancers or
potential employees who possess the skills
and expertise needed to fulfill the tasks
you want to outsource. Utilize platforms
like Upwork, Freelancer, or Fiverr to find
qualified freelancers, or leverage
professional networks and job boards to
find suitable employees. Review portfolios,
resumes, or work samples to ensure they
align with your requirements and
standards.

Establish Clear Communication: Effective communication is crucial when outsourcing tasks or working with a remote team. Clearly communicate your expectations, project requirements, deadlines, and desired outcomes. Utilize communication tools like email, project management platforms, or video conferencing to maintain regular and transparent communication with your team members.

Provide Detailed Guidelines and Training: When outsourcing tasks, provide detailed guidelines, templates, and instructions to ensure consistency and quality. If specific processes or procedures need to be followed, provide clear documentation or conduct training sessions to familiarize team members with your affiliate marketing business and its unique requirements. Regularly check in with team members to address any questions or concerns they may have.

Maintain Quality Control: While outsourcing tasks, it's essential to maintain quality control over the work being produced. Establish quality standards and review the work of your team members regularly. Provide constructive feedback and guidance to ensure that the output meets your expectations. This helps maintain the integrity of your brand and ensures a consistent experience for your audience.

Foster a Positive Team Culture: Whether you're working with freelancers or building a team of employees, fostering a positive team culture is crucial for collaboration and productivity. Encourage open communication, provide recognition for a job well done, and foster a supportive and inclusive work environment. Regularly check in with your team members to ensure their needs are met and address any concerns promptly.

Evaluate Performance and Adjust as Needed: Continuously assess the performance of your team members and the effectiveness of outsourcing certain tasks. Monitor key metrics, such as productivity, quality, and timeliness of deliverables. Address any performance issues or bottlenecks promptly and make adjustments as needed. Regularly evaluate the return on investment (ROI) of outsourcing and the impact on your business goals.

Protect Intellectual Property and Confidentiality: When working with freelancers or team members, ensure that appropriate confidentiality agreements or non-disclosure agreements are in place to protect your intellectual property and sensitive business information. Clearly define ownership rights and ensure that all parties understand and adhere to these agreements.

Outsourcing tasks and building a team can significantly enhance your efficiency, productivity, and scalability in affiliate marketing. By leveraging the skills and expertise of others, you can focus on strategic activities that drive your business forward. Effective communication, clear guidelines, and quality control mechanisms are essential for successful outsourcing. Regularly evaluate performance, make adjustments as needed, and foster a positive team culture to create a cohesive and productive team environment.

Expanding into New Markets and Niches

Expanding into new markets and niches is a strategic step to grow your affiliate marketing business and tap into additional sources of revenue. By identifying and targeting new audiences, you can increase your reach and diversify your income streams. ***Here are some considerations when expanding into new markets and niches***:

Conduct Market Research: Start by conducting thorough market research to identify potential new markets and niches. Look for emerging trends, gaps in the market, or underserved audiences. Analyze the demand, competition, and profitability of the new market segments to assess their viability.

Evaluate Fit with Your Expertise: Assess whether the new markets and niches align with your existing expertise, resources, and interests. Consider your knowledge, skills, and experience in relation to the target market. It's crucial to have a genuine interest and understanding of the new market to effectively cater to the needs and preferences of your audience.

Define Your Unique Selling Proposition (USP): Determine your unique value proposition for the new market. Identify what sets you apart from competitors and how you can offer something distinctive and valuable to the target audience. Your USP could be specialized knowledge, unique content, superior customer service, or innovative solutions that address specific pain points.

Adapt Your Marketing Strategy: Tailor your marketing strategy to resonate with the new market segment. Research their preferences, behaviors, and communication channels. Customize your messaging, branding, and promotional efforts to effectively engage and attract the attention of the new audience. Consider language, cultural nuances, and local market dynamics to ensure your marketing efforts are relevant and impactful.

Develop Relevant Content: Create content that specifically targets the new market segment. Generate informative, engaging, and valuable content that addresses their specific needs, challenges, and interests. Use keyword research and SEO techniques to optimize your content for the new market's search queries and drive organic traffic.

Build Relationships and Networks:
Establish connections with influencers, bloggers, and industry experts within the new market segment. Collaborate on guest blogging, joint ventures, or promotional activities to leverage their existing networks and gain exposure to the new audience. Engage with communities, forums, and social media groups where the target audience congregates to build relationships and establish your presence.

Test and Refine Your Approach: Begin by testing your expansion efforts on a smaller scale before fully committing your resources. Experiment with different marketing channels, strategies, and offerings to gauge the response and gather feedback from the new market segment. Continuously monitor and analyze the results to identify what works well and make adjustments as needed.

Adapt Your Affiliate Partnerships: Evaluate your existing affiliate partnerships and explore new ones that align with the interests and preferences of the new market. Look for affiliate programs that offer relevant products or services catering to the specific needs of the target audience. Ensure the commission structures and payout methods are favorable and support your growth objectives.

Monitor Performance and Metrics: Regularly track and analyze key performance indicators (KPIs) to measure the success of your expansion efforts. Monitor metrics such as traffic, conversions, sales, and affiliate earnings in the new market segment. Use analytics tools and reports provided by affiliate networks to gain insights into the effectiveness of your strategies and identify areas for improvement.

Adapt and Iterate: Stay flexible and adaptable in your approach as you expand into new markets and niches. Monitor market trends, consumer preferences, and industry dynamics to identify opportunities and adjust your strategies accordingly. Continuously learn, iterate, and refine your approach based on the feedback and data you gather.

Expanding into new markets and niches requires careful planning, research, and targeted marketing efforts. By understanding the unique needs of the new audience, adapting your strategies, and consistently delivering value, you can successfully penetrate new markets and unlock additional growth opportunities for your affiliate marketing business.

Keeping up with Industry Trends and Changes

In the dynamic world of affiliate marketing, staying up-to-date with industry trends and changes is essential for maintaining a competitive edge and adapting to evolving market conditions. **Here are some strategies to help you effectively keep up with industry trends and changes**:

Follow Industry Publications and Blogs: Subscribe to reputable industry publications, blogs, and newsletters that provide insights, news, and analysis related to affiliate marketing. Stay informed about the latest trends, best practices, and emerging technologies.

Regularly read articles, case studies, and thought leadership pieces to broaden your knowledge and gain valuable industry insights.

Attend Industry Conferences and Events: Participate in affiliate marketing conferences, seminars, webinars, and networking events. These events offer opportunities to connect with industry experts, learn from keynote speakers, and engage in discussions about the latest trends and developments. Take notes, ask questions, and network with fellow professionals to exchange ideas and stay informed about the latest industry happenings.

Engage in Online Communities and Forums: Join online communities, forums, and social media groups focused on affiliate marketing. Participate in discussions, ask questions, and share your insights. Engaging with like-minded professionals allows you to stay updated on industry trends, exchange knowledge, and learn from others' experiences. Platforms such as Reddit, Facebook groups, and specialized forums can be valuable sources of information and networking opportunities.

Follow Influencers and Thought Leaders: Identify influential figures in the affiliate marketing industry and follow them on social media platforms like Twitter, LinkedIn, and YouTube. Pay attention to their content, insights, and recommendations. Influencers often share valuable tips, strategies, and updates about industry trends. Engaging with them by commenting, sharing, or asking questions can also help you build relationships within the industry.

Leverage Webinars and Online Courses: Attend webinars and online courses focused on affiliate marketing. Many industry experts and organizations offer webinars and educational programs covering a wide range of topics, from beginner-level concepts to advanced strategies. These resources can provide you with valuable insights, practical tips, and the latest information about industry trends and changes.

Monitor Industry News and Updates: Regularly check industry news websites, forums, and social media channels for updates on affiliate marketing trends, algorithm changes, policy updates, and new regulations. Set up Google Alerts or use RSS feed readers to receive notifications about relevant keywords or topics related to affiliate marketing. Stay informed about the latest news to anticipate shifts in the industry and proactively adapt your strategies.

Network with Peers and Industry Professionals: Attend industry networking events, join online communities, and connect with fellow affiliate marketers.

Networking provides opportunities to share experiences, exchange ideas, and learn from others in the field. Building relationships with peers and industry professionals can lead to valuable insights, collaborations, and mutual support in navigating industry changes.

Analyze Data and Metrics: Regularly analyze your own data and performance metrics to identify patterns, trends, and areas for improvement. Pay attention to key performance indicators (KPIs) such as conversion rates, click-through rates, traffic sources, and affiliate earnings. By understanding your own data, you can spot emerging trends, make data-driven decisions, and adapt your strategies accordingly.

Embrace Continuous Learning: Develop a mindset of continuous learning and improvement. Seek out educational resources such as books, podcasts, and online courses that cover various aspects of affiliate marketing. Stay curious and open to new ideas, concepts, and strategies. By continuously expanding your knowledge, you'll be better equipped to identify industry trends and adapt to changes effectively.

Stay Agile and Adapt Quickly: The affiliate marketing landscape can change rapidly. Be prepared to pivot and adapt your strategies based on industry trends, consumer behavior, and technological advancements. Embrace experimentation, test new approaches, and be willing to adjust your tactics as needed. Agility and adaptability are key to thriving in a dynamic industry.

By actively staying informed about industry trends and changes, you can position yourself as a knowledgeable and adaptable affiliate marketer.

Continuously learning, networking, and monitoring the industry landscape will enable you to seize opportunities, stay ahead of the competition, and drive success in your affiliate marketing endeavors.

Continuous Learning and Professional Development

In the rapidly evolving field of affiliate marketing, continuous learning and professional development are essential for staying competitive, expanding your knowledge, and refining your skills. By investing in your ongoing education, you can adapt to industry changes, explore new strategies, and enhance your expertise.

Here are some key aspects to consider when it comes to continuous learning and professional development:

Stay Updated with Industry Trends: Stay abreast of the latest industry trends, technological advancements, and best practices. Follow industry publications, blogs, podcasts, and social media channels to access valuable insights, case studies, and thought leadership content. Engage in discussions and attend industry conferences to gain exposure to new ideas and perspectives.

Expand Your Knowledge Base: Seek out learning opportunities that cover various aspects of affiliate marketing, including but not limited to SEO, content creation, social media marketing, email marketing, analytics, and conversion optimization. Take advantage of online courses, webinars, workshops, and certifications offered by reputable organizations and industry experts.

Networking and Collaboration: Connect with fellow affiliate marketers, industry professionals, and influencers. Engage in online communities, forums, and social media groups to exchange knowledge, share experiences, and learn from others. Networking provides opportunities for collaboration, partnership, and mentorship, allowing you to benefit from the collective wisdom of the affiliate marketing community.

Attend Conferences and Events: Participate in affiliate marketing conferences, seminars, and workshops. These events offer valuable learning opportunities, networking possibilities, and access to industry leaders and experts. Attend sessions, panel discussions, and keynote speeches to gain insights into emerging trends, strategies, and success stories. Take advantage of the chance to meet industry influencers and build connections.

Experiment and Test: Embrace a mindset of experimentation and testing. Implement new strategies, tools, and techniques and evaluate their effectiveness. A willingness to try new approaches allows you to gather data, identify what works best for your audience and niche, and make informed decisions based on results.

Leverage Online Resources: Explore online resources such as blogs, podcasts, and YouTube channels dedicated to affiliate marketing. Subscribe to newsletters and join communities to receive regular updates, insights, and tips from industry experts. These resources often provide practical advice, case studies, and real-world examples that can enhance your understanding and skill set.

Analyze and Optimize Performance: Regularly analyze your performance metrics, such as click-through rates, conversion rates, and revenue generated, to identify areas for improvement.

Utilize analytics tools and platforms to gain insights into user behavior, demographics, and engagement patterns. Use these insights to optimize your strategies and campaigns.

Develop Soft Skills: Affiliate marketing requires not only technical expertise but also strong communication, negotiation, and relationship-building skills. Invest in developing your soft skills, including effective communication, time management, problem-solving, and leadership. These skills will help you build better relationships with affiliate partners, advertisers, and your audience.

Seek Feedback and Mentorship: Actively seek feedback from your audience, peers, and mentors. Request constructive criticism and suggestions for improvement. Consider finding a mentor who can provide guidance, share insights, and offer support as you navigate your affiliate marketing journey.

Their experience and perspective can help you grow both personally and professionally.

Set Goals and Measure Progress: Establish specific goals for your professional development and track your progress. Regularly assess your achievements, identify areas where you need further improvement, and set new targets. This approach ensures you are continually challenging yourself, expanding your skill set, and advancing your career in affiliate marketing.

Remember, continuous learning and professional development are ongoing processes. Embrace a growth mindset, remain curious, and stay adaptable to navigate the ever-changing landscape of affiliate marketing. By investing in your own growth and development, you'll position yourself for long-term success in the field.

Adapting Your Strategies to the Evolving Landscape

In the fast-paced and ever-changing world of affiliate marketing, it is crucial to adapt your strategies to the evolving landscape. Market trends, consumer behavior, and technology advancements continually shape the affiliate marketing industry. *Here are some key considerations for adapting your strategies*:

Stay Current with Industry Updates: Regularly monitor industry news, publications, blogs, and forums to stay informed about the latest developments and trends in affiliate marketing. Subscribe to newsletters, follow industry influencers, and engage in discussions to gain insights into emerging strategies and changing consumer preferences.

Analyze Data and Metrics: Continuously analyze your data and performance metrics to understand the effectiveness of your current strategies. Identify patterns, trends, and areas for improvement. By leveraging analytics tools, you can gain valuable insights into user behavior, conversion rates, traffic sources, and campaign performance. Use this data to make informed decisions and adjust your strategies accordingly.

Embrace Technological Advancements: Keep up with technological advancements that impact affiliate marketing. Explore new tools, platforms, and software that can enhance your marketing efforts. For example, consider leveraging artificial intelligence (AI) for personalized recommendations, automation tools for streamlined processes, or mobile optimization for improved user experiences.

Embracing technology can give you a competitive edge and enable you to reach your target audience more effectively.

Monitor Consumer Behavior: Pay close attention to shifts in consumer behavior and preferences. Stay attuned to changes in their needs, expectations, and purchasing patterns. By understanding your audience, you can tailor your strategies to deliver the right message, at the right time, and through the right channels. Consider conducting market research, surveys, and user testing to gather insights directly from your target audience.

Experiment and Test: Adopt a mindset of experimentation and testing. Be willing to try new approaches, strategies, and promotional channels. Conduct A/B tests to compare different variations of your campaigns, landing pages, or messaging.

Test different marketing channels, content formats, and promotional offers to discover what resonates best with your audience. Continuously evaluate the results and refine your strategies based on data-driven insights.

Focus on User Experience: The user experience plays a critical role in affiliate marketing success. Ensure that your website, landing pages, and content are optimized for a seamless and engaging user experience. Consider factors such as page load speed, mobile responsiveness, intuitive navigation, and compelling visuals. A positive user experience can boost engagement, increase conversions, and foster long-term relationships with your audience.

Adapt to Regulatory Changes: Stay informed about regulatory changes and compliance requirements relevant to affiliate marketing.

Understand the rules and guidelines set forth by regulatory bodies, such as the Federal Trade Commission (FTC), to ensure transparency, fair practices, and proper disclosure of affiliate relationships. Compliance with regulations not only protects your business but also builds trust with your audience.

Monitor Competitor Strategies: Keep an eye on your competitors' strategies and tactics. Monitor their promotional efforts, content strategies, and partnerships. Identify what is working well for them and consider how you can differentiate yourself and offer unique value to your audience. This analysis can inspire new ideas, highlight potential gaps in the market, and help you refine your own strategies.

Engage in Continuous Learning: Invest in your own professional development by continuously learning and expanding your knowledge. Attend industry conferences, participate in webinars, and take advantage of educational resources to stay updated on industry best practices and new trends. By staying current, you can proactively adapt your strategies to align with the evolving landscape.

Seek Feedback and Adapt Accordingly: Actively seek feedback from your audience, partners, and industry peers. Encourage open communication and listen to their suggestions, comments, and concerns. Use this feedback to refine your strategies, improve user experiences, and address any areas that may need adjustment. Continuous improvement based on feedback is key to adapting your strategies effectively.

Adapting your strategies to the evolving landscape requires a proactive and flexible approach. By staying informed, analyzing data, understanding your audience, and embracing changes, you can stay ahead of the curve and drive success in the dynamic world of affiliate marketing.